What clients and colleagues say about the authors. . .

"Kathy Thebo is an inspiration and a born salesperson who can captivate an audience of one or one thousand. It's hard to believe she was once shy."
—Jeannette Reddish Scollard, entrepreneur, lecturer, author, *The Self-Employed Woman*

"The wonderful thing about working with Joyce Newman is that not only does she make one's communication skills sharper and more effective, she also gets you to enjoy the entire process of getting up before a room and speaking or being interviewed by a member of the press. The name of her book should be *The Joy of Communication* and Joyce is certainly the perfect author."
—Joseph J. Esposito, president, Encyclopedia Brittanica Publishing Group

"Kathy can sell herself and she has taught others to do the same, both as a keynote speaker and in her terrific book, *Selling Yourself*."
—Susan Bixler, author, *Professional Presence*

"Joyce Newman has a unique talent for bringing out the best in people, particularly in helping them be more persuasive and powerful in 'command' situations, such as speeches and press interviews."
—William Stasior, chairman and CEO, Booz•Allen Hamilton Inc.

"As a business owner, I know that confidence can make or break a deal...can mean the difference between success and failure. Kathy Thebo writes not just from experience but from the heart."
—Beverly Duran, CEO, The Retail Consultant Group

"Joyce Newman is a miracle worker. She has made many Bear Stearns executives with little or no public speaking experience 'come alive' as a result of her coaching. This book is a must for anyone who needs speech or presentation training."
>—Hannah Burns, managing director of corporate communications, Bear, Stearns & Co. Inc.

"Kathy is a shining example of overcoming adversity through dedicated goal setting. Her story has meaning for millions of people who suffer from the dilemma of low self-esteem."
>—Clarence O. Smith, president, *Essence*

"Joyce packs a soft punch, increasing your confidence without sacrificing honesty. One of our managers described her this way: 'A session with Joyce is a lifetime of speaking confidence.' "
>—Anthony Pucillo, vice president of sales, industrial and commercial lighting, Osram Sylvania Inc.

"When I first met Kathy Thebo, I didn't realize she was 'selling herself' to me. Instead, I concluded she was a wonderfully competent, confident entrepreneur with a great story to tell other women who are struggling to achieve success. I believe that now more than ever."
>—John Mack Carter, editor-in-chief, *Good Housekeeping*

"Joyce decrees doctorates of confidence on those about to embark upon the unknown. She helped me prepare for my book tour quickly, skillfully, and painlessly. This book should do the same for you."
>—Hal F. Rosenbluth, president and CEO, Rosenbluth International, author, *The Customer Comes Second*

"Kathy is a true believer in the concept that 'all we send into the lives of others comes back into our own.' She always gives that extra little bit to her customers and friends."
>—Nina Harris, author and professional speaker

"Joyce is a communications magician. She illustrates how to consistently draw positive skills out of the hat, and keep any negative ones up your sleeve. Whenever I'm 'on stage'—speaking before a group, or in a meeting—I am more confident than ever, thanks to Joyce."
—Millie Martini Bratten, executive editor,
Bride's and *Your New Home*

"Kathy's winning combination of an open, sincere personality, sense of style, and insight into color and accessories create an environment of beauty for every client. She knows how to embellish your good features and diminish the imperfections...She's a gem."
—Elaine S. Cohen, operations supervisor,
U.S. Department of Health and Human Services

"As a public relations specialist in book publishing, I have turned to Joyce Newman to help authors articulate their thoughts and communicate their message with clarity and confidence...she has always performed brilliantly in preparing them for battle!"
—Nancy Kahan, author, *Entertaining for Business*

"Selling is a unique skill and Kathy is unique in the selling arena. Now she teaches others by example and experience."
—Kathy Borders, advertising manager,
Arizona Capitol Times

"For a woman in the public eye, what counts is her appearance—her ability to look smart and sound smart. The cut of her hair. The color of her makeup. The way a woman speaks and presents herself all contribute to her confidence and authority. Joyce understands the power of image—and how a woman can put it all together."
—Dorothy Schefer, deputy editor, *Mirabella*

"Kathy Thebo is a truly delightful woman who knows her business well and treats each of her clients in a refreshing, confident manner. No 'hard sell' here...always a pleasure!"
—Joan Brainard, director,
Phoenix YWCA Senior Center

"Although a seasoned public speaker, the talk show/media circuit to promote my book intimidated me—that is, until I met Joyce Newman. As a result of her step-by-step coaching, my experiences with the media have been remarkably easy. Joyce not only increased my confidence...she increased book sales!"
—Michelle Weiner-Davis, author, *Divorce Busting*

"Kathy Thebo's quiet strength and confidence are evidenced through her ability to build a successful business while maintaining her sense of humor and friendliness. She's innovative, polished, professional, and organized. We all benefit!"
—Cathy Doyle, administrator, Pheonix Orthopedic
Surgeons and Sports Medicine Institute

"It's one thing to know what to say. It's quite another to say it effectively. Joyce has a wonderful knack to turn content into persuasion."
—William D. Novelli, executive vice president, CARE

"As Kathy's fifth grade teacher, it makes me very proud to see that timid girl blossom into a self-assured and confident businessperson and public speaker. *Selling Yourself* is full of advice anyone can use to present a more polished and charismatic appearance."
—Lucy Re, teacher, actress, singer, and dancer

"Joyce has brought out the best in many of our authors. When we send a Joyce Newman–trained author to an interview, we know they will be a terrific spokesperson. And our media contacts know they will have a fabulous show or article."
—Meryl Zegarek, associate director of publicity,
William Morrow & Company Inc.

Selling Yourself

Selling Yourself

Be The Competent, Confident Person You Really Are!

Kathy Thebo & Joyce Newman

MasterMedia Limited
New York

Published 1994 by MasterMedia Limited

MASTERMEDIA and colophon are registered trademarks of MasterMedia Limited.

Library of Congress Cataloging-in-Publication Data
Thebo, Kathy.
    Selling yourself : be the competent, confident person you really are! / Kathy Thebo, Joyce Newman.
            p.   cm.
    ISBN 0-942361-80-6 (pbk.) : $12.95
    1. Self-confidence. 2. Success. 3. Persuasion (Psychology)
4. Business communication. I. Newman, Joyce. II. Title.
BF575.S39T54   1994
650.1—dc20   94-3065

Book design and production services by
Lynn & Turek Productions, New York,
with thanks to Michael and Alan.

Manufactured in the United States of America

DEDICATIONS

In fond memory of Isabelle Hallows, my mother.
To Mike, Ivy, John, and Mary Kate, my dear children.
Thank you, Bill, for your love and support.
With love to Mary and Charles Thebo.
To my Aunt Mary and my father's sisters,
who are also precious to me.

~Kathy

To my daughter, Wendi Rachel Newman,
with love and admiration.
And to my husband, Richard,
who has always believed in me and
gives me constant support and encouragement,
both in business and in life.

~Joyce

CONTENTS

Introduction   *xv*

Part One: Your Personal Impact

1.   The Right Foot:
      Unforgettable First Impressions   3

2.   Personal Presence:
      Cultivating Charisma   15

3.   A Touch of Polish:
      Contemporary Etiquette for the Professional   25

Part Two: Selling Yourself

4.   The Power of Persuasion:
      Interpersonal Communication Skills   57

5.   Let's Make A Deal:
      The Art and Science of Selling   81

6.   Blow Your Own Horn:
      Ten Techniques for Successful Self-Promotion   107

CONTENTS

7. The Perfect Pitch:
    Creating Press Releases Like a Pro *129*

8. Meet the Press:
    Strategies for Mastering the Media *149*

9. Center Stage:
    Delivering Powerful Speeches and Presentations *175*

Part Three: Assessing Your Life and Your Style

10. Style vs. Substance:
    Projecting an Image that Reveals the Real You *205*

11. Stop the Clock:
    Managing Your Time and Your Life *241*

12. Do What You Love:
    Are You an Entrepreneur at Heart? *271*

    About the Authors *293*

ACKNOWLEDGMENTS

WITH LOVE TO MY MOTHER AND FATHER, ISABELLE AND KEN Hallows. Thank you for my life and for my brothers and sisters: Ken, Jim, Randy, Terry, Bob, Nancy, Patti, Kevin, and John. Thank you for teaching us the importance of always giving more than we receive.

Special thanks to my best friends, Sherry Schroeder and Darsel Minter, who have been with me from the beginning.

Thank you to all my friends at Avon who believed in me and helped me realize my full potential, especially Rose Kenyon, Ginny Macy, Barbara Janes, Jim Preston, Walker Lewis, Pat Woods, Barbara Knizner, Nancy Glaser, Gail Blanke, Alix Mendes, Kathleen Walas, Morgan Hare, Suzanne Bronski, Claudia Poccia, Dennis Dunn, Maria Montoya, Debbie Reale, and Brenda Henning. Thank you, Carolyn Aishton, for "discovering" me on the Mississippi Queen and guiding me on the path to success. You have been a true friend!

With sincere appreciation to Susan Stautberg and Diana Lynn for their dedication and hard work on this project.

Most of all, sincere gratitude to all my wonderful customers who have become my dear friends—to them I truly owe my "metamorphosis"!

—*Kathy Thebo*

ACKNOWLEDGMENTS

SPECIAL THANKS TO MY FRIENDS AND PUBLIC RELATIONS professionals, who were always willing to take the time to share their wisdom and experience: Phyllis Berlowe, Sheila Kelley, Bill Novelli, Barbara Taylor, Wes Truesdell, and Richard Weiner.

Thanks also to Rona and John Roberts, who have always been there.

Thank you to Susan Stautberg, whose creativity and tenacity helped make this book a reality.

And a very special thank you to Diana Lynn, who took the time and devoted her energy and talent to making *Selling Yourself* the best it could be.

—*Joyce Newman*

INTRODUCTION

WHEN WE FIRST TOLD FRIENDS AND COLLEAGUES ABOUT *Selling Yourself,* more than one raised an eyebrow and joked about our motives for writing a book on the "world's oldest profession." Their jesting confirmed our premise: "selling" is a dirty word in many people's minds. Asked to visualize a typical salesman, many of us conjure up images of sleazy characters conniving to get the best of us and our pocketbooks.

The fact is, we all do a little selling every day. Most of us just don't realize it. If you've ever tried to persuade a child to go to bed early, urge an acquaintance to volunteer for a committee, or convince a spouse with a taste for meat and potatoes to try a new ethnic restaurant, in that moment, you were selling something—your point of view. And anyone who's ever gone on a job interview was definitely in the business of pitching a product—themselves.

The point is, selling is an inescapable reality in our daily lives, and it's becoming an increasingly critical skill for professional success. Corporate downsizing and the reconfiguration of American business are spawning innovative work arrangements, such as job sharing and telecommuting, that were virtually unheard of a decade ago. At the same time, the growing ranks of the unemployed are giving birth to a new breed of entrepreneur: people who are reluctantly facing the realization that traditional job security is a thing of the past.

Introduction

We live in a fast-paced world that continues to grow more complex and competitive. To keep up, many of us find that the lines between our personal and professional lives are continually crossing, creating the added pressure of always "being on." We can't afford not to put our best foot forward—every day and in all kinds of situations—because we never know when we might have a chance to meet our next client or make a contact that could prove critical to our future.

That's what *Selling Yourself* is all about: learning how to project a polished, confident image that will help open doors to new opportunities and dreams.

Whether you want to make a good impression in social settings, establish a reputation as a dynamic leader in your community or profession, or build a business, we believe *Selling Yourself* can help. As entrepreneurs—Kathy is an award-winning sales representative and Joyce is one of the country's foremost media trainers and communications consultants—we've made our share of mistakes, but we've also learned many lessons that proved valuable to our success.

You'll discover them in the following pages, for *Selling Yourself* is loaded with tried-and-true techniques that will help you have a more powerful impact. Wish you were more charismatic? We'll show you how to cultivate charisma—and why appearance isn't nearly as important as your ability to create a "presence." Does the thought of entering a room full of strangers set your knees to quivering? Not to worry. We'll share a few tricks sure to help you mingle with ease. Hoping to make headlines with your new business? We'll teach you how to deal with the press like a pro. From insights on time management to tips on public speaking, *Selling Yourself* aims to equip you with the skills and self-confidence you need to face the world with poise and assurance.

So start polishing your image now. Don't wait for that promotion, or an important interview, or an invitation to speak before a civic or professional group. Many small changes you can make today will add up to big successes tomorrow!

PART ONE

Your Personal Impact

THE RIGHT FOOT:
Unforgettable First Impressions

> *You never get a second chance
> to make a first impression.*
> —Anonymous

> *First impressions can be effective or
> disastrous, but they are always lasting.*
> —Susan Bixler
> *Professional Presence*

THE FAMILIAR ADAGE ABOUT SECOND CHANCES AND FIRST impressions has never been more on target than in today's fast-paced world, where our professional and personal lives routinely mix. This is especially true if you, like us, make your living as an entrepreneur. By nature and necessity, entrepreneurs are salespeople. The success of their ventures invariably depends on finding customers for their products or services. For these professionals, every meeting, each introduction—even a chance encounter—is an opportunity to forge a bond that could lead to future business.

Even people whose professions don't involve marketing per se are becoming painfully aware that the ability to sell oneself and one's skills is essential in today's economy. With almost every industry imaginable retooling and businesses downsizing right and left, it's no longer realistic for most people to anchor their identities to a single job title. Career experts claim the average worker will change jobs at least eight times in his or her lifetime—and change careers at least three times.

That projection certainly seems credible in light of the many news accounts of plant closings and companies going bust in recent years. Think about the number of stories you've read or heard in which workers who thought they were secure in their careers suddenly faced the prospect of dusting off their résumés, polishing their interviewing skills, and plunging back into the job market.

Whether by choice or circumstances, we all encounter situations that require savvy selling—even if we don't recognize them as such. "When the word 'salesperson' comes up, many people still automatically think of the stereotypical used car salesperson, insurance salesperson, or door-to-door salesperson," says Terry Booton, a veteran salesman and author of *Cracking New Accounts*. But the fact is, we are all salespeople to some extent, says Booton, who cites these examples:

- Parents sell their children on why they need to eat certain foods or act in a certain manner.
- Doctors sell their patients on why they need to take certain drugs or undergo surgery.
- Lawyers sell when presenting cases to a judge or jury.
- Accountants sell when they try to convince their clients to make an investment for tax purposes.

- Waiters and waitresses sell when they offer you those scrumptious desserts after dinner.
- Teachers sell students on why courses are important.

Whatever the situation, people who successfully sell have one thing in common: confidence. They believe in what they're trying to sell, and they're confident they can convince you to believe it too. That's why the ability to project a competent, confident image is one of the most valuable skills you can develop.

Your image influences every aspect of your life. Professional or personal, your relationships are determined largely by the image you project. Too often, either because we're busy, caught off guard, or simply preoccupied with other thoughts, we underestimate the value of starting off on the right foot when we first meet someone.

It pays to heed the age-old counsel on first impressions—because every second counts. Studies show that people size up each other in the first three to five seconds of an encounter. Within thirty seconds, at least eleven assumptions are made about the other person, including social and economic status; educational attainment; occupation; trustworthiness and credibility; marital status; and ancestry. Though the process is an unconscious one, this mental categorizing is an all-important first step in continuing any kind of association—whether you're at a business meeting or a neighbor's backyard barbecue. Understanding the dynamics of first impressions can make the difference between becoming a victim of snap judgments and successfully managing your image and impact on others.

CREATE YOUR OWN HALO

Sociologists have dubbed the ability to make a positive and unforgettably powerful first impression within the first thirty seconds of meeting someone as the "halo effect." First impressions are formed through an intricate combination of visual and vocal cues, including your appearance and appropriateness of dress, your manners and mannerisms, the firmness of your handshake, your ability to maintain eye contact, your posture, the amount of space you maintain between yourself and the other person, when you speak and the tone of voice you use. Even when you don't say a word, your image can speak volumes.

The halo effect is easy to create with a few simple steps, say Linda and Wayne Phillips in their book *The Concise Guide to Executive Etiquette.* Their advice:

- *Always rise* (this includes women executives).
- *Always shake the hand* of the person to whom you're being introduced.
- *Smile* cordially and say, "How do you do?" As a memory aid, repeat the person's name: "How do you do, Mr. Miller?" Save "I'm very glad to meet you" for the times when you are truly sincere—meeting someone you've heard a great deal about, someone whose work has influenced your own, and so forth. Otherwise, "How do you do" is sufficient. Then pick up the conversation clue that the person introducing you should have provided and carry on from there.

PACKAGING YOUR IMAGE

Image is the silent introduction of ourselves to others. Whenever we walk into a room, our clothing, personal grooming, and body language are immediately on display. While you might argue that this kind of superficial scrutiny is insufficient to size up the whole human being that you are, there's no denying such judgments. Research shows that job applicants who effectively project a professional image command higher starting salaries—as much as twenty percent more—than those who do not.

While experts say it's all but impossible to erase a bad impression if you start off on the wrong foot, making a great first impression isn't that hard if you understand some basic ground rules.

Dress The Part

It's not our intent to offer a formulaic dress code. Rather, we want to raise your awareness of how dressing smartly, whatever the occasion, is one way you can influence first impressions. Researchers have found that people are most often attracted to mirror images of themselves. In other words, when someone is dressed similarly to us, we automatically infer from their appearance that they also have similar beliefs, values and attitudes—even the same political affiliations.

This knowledge can be used effectively in all kinds of situations. For instance, Joyce's clients include authors who come to her for coaching before embarking on national book tours involving television appearances. She "packages their image" by teaching them the power that clothing and personal grooming have to create different impressions, and by working with them to achieve a look that supports the particular image they want to project.

Likewise, journalists, especially beginning reporters, receive a variation of this advice from their editors and producers. While most people have the good sense not to show up for an interview with the governor dressed in shorts and a T-shirt, cub reporters may not realize it's equally foolhardy to wear a suit and tie or high heels to an interview with a farmer who's losing his crops to drought.

Inappropriate attire can create unnecessary obstacles by becoming the focus of your encounter. Or, as famed fashion designer Coco Chanel once said: "If a woman is poorly dressed, you notice her dress, and if she is impeccably dressed, you notice the woman." Many people interpret appropriate attire as a sign of respect—for yourself and for the person with whom you're dealing.

Imagine the impression that over-dressed reporter makes on the farmer. At best, it's an uncomfortable situation. But the real risk is that the reporter will lose credibility with this source. Think about it. If you were the farmer, how willing would you be to talk freely with someone who clearly doesn't understand the first thing about your environment, let alone your problems?

Dress is the outer expression of the inner person, and in most situations, you can expect to be judged accordingly. Dressing the part by adapting your physical appearance to the circumstances or the requirements of the other person can enhance your credibility, help build rapport, and may ultimately increase your chances for success—whether you're trying to sell your services to a new client, convince a prospective employer you're the right person for the job, or make a good impression on a new acquaintance. We'll explore the matter of dress more fully in our chapter on personal style, but here's a quick technique you can employ right away to help improve your first impressions.

The 30-Second Detail Check

Corporate image consultant Susan Bixler has developed what she calls the "30-second detail check" to guard against grooming gaffes such as spinach caught in a tooth, which, although not disastrous, can be distracting enough to diminish your impact.

"No pilot takes off without doing a visual check of the plane to make sure everything is A-OK. No scuba diver jumps off a boat without making sure that the air valves are working," Bixler writes in her book *Professional Presence.* "And no businessperson should walk into a business meeting without making the detail check."

The benefits of this spot check are twofold. The first, obviously, is to prevent an embarrassing faux pas. Equally important, by giving yourself this extra reassurance, "you'll be able to walk into any room, hold out your hand, and concentrate on the people and business present," Bixler says.

Bixler's detail check, step by step:

✔Find a restroom and start at the top. Check your hair, teeth, makeup, and earrings. Thousands of women run around all day vaguely aware that they have on only one earring. The other is next to their phone.

✔Secure your scarf or straighten your tie.

✔Check for dandruff, stains, and open buttons.

✔Put your jacket on—buttoned for formality, unbuttoned for a friendlier look. Remember: we're seen more from the waist up, because we spend more time seated.

MAKING FIRST IMPRESSIONS WORK FOR YOU

When meeting new people, particularly in business situations, our objective is usually to create rapport and establish a comfortable level of trust. You want to come across as warm and friendly, without appearing to flirt or be overly familiar, and to exude an air of self-assurance and poise, without seeming stiff or unapproachable. Striking this balance isn't always easy in thirty seconds (remember, we're talking about first impressions).

You might be surprised to know that what you say when you meet someone isn't nearly as important as how you say it. In fact, of the three elements that have been determined to influence first impressions, words account for only seven percent, whereas vocal quality accounts for thirty-five percent. More than fifty percent of an initial impression is based on silent signals—nonverbal communication, which includes body language and appearance.

Gestures, facial expressions, and tone of voice all can enhance your image and improve a first impression, as long as they match the message you're trying to send. For example, it's hard to convey genuine interest when welcoming someone to a gathering, if you have a deadpan delivery while introducing that person to other guests. Body language, such as twirling your hair or tapping your foot, can be a telltale signal that you're not fully engaged in the events at hand.

By the same token, confident body language can effectively disguise inner nervousness. For instance, the less you gesticulate, the more powerful you'll appear. Enter a room with energy, stride purposefully to your destination with head held high and back straight, and you'll come across as sure-footed and self-assured.

Body language is such an integral part of communication and creating a confident image that we will address it many times throughout this book. For now, here are a couple of simple, straightforward techniques to keep in mind when you want to make a positive first impression.

Eye Contact

Poetically characterized as "windows to the soul," our eyes can express a wide array of messages, from enthusiasm and admiration to boredom and displeasure. Properly used, eye contact can be one of your strongest communication tools.

"The amount of eye contact deemed appropriate varies greatly from culture to culture," says international image consultant Hilka Klinkenberg. "Here in the United States, polite eye contact ranges from 40 percent to 60 percent of the time. Less than that, and you may appear shifty, devious, or untrustworthy," she says. Conversely, making eye contact more than 60 percent of the time creates the impression you're imperious, authoritarian, and intimidating.

In her book *At Ease...Professionally,* Klinkenberg advises, "When you are speaking to people, you may want to pay close attention to their eyes to see if you are holding their attention. If not, you may want to adjust your style of communication and possibly ask a question to get them to speak and to refocus their attention."

Physical Contact

A ritual of American business and common practice in many social settings, the handshake is often a crucial clasp. It sets the tone for the immediate encounter, and it may well determine the fate of any future relationship. Many people actually believe they can sense the true measure of another person by the quality of the handshake they share.

Yet so many people, men and women, don't know how to shake hands. And this can be surprisingly disconcerting, even disappointing, according to Joyce, who remembers her reaction upon trading handshakes with a man whose career she had admired for many years.

"I couldn't wait to meet him. And then he gave me this limp, halfhearted handshake. I was so taken aback—this man was one of my heroes—that I thought 'No, I imagined it.' So at the end of the meeting, I went up to him to say good-bye, and he did it again. Unfortunately, it told me something about him that I didn't want to know: he was a cold fish, not at all the 'people person' I had expected."

Handshake How-Tos

A handshake should be strong and accompanied by a smile and direct eye contact. We cannot overemphasize the importance of meeting someone eye to eye at this moment.

Other handshake how-tos:
> ✔When visiting someone's office or environment, wait momentarily for your host to offer

his or her hand. If it appears no handshake is forthcoming, extend your hand. Some experts advise that no important business meeting should start without a handshake.

✔A handshake should last about three seconds and involve the whole hand, not just the fingertips. Grasp the other person's hand, palm to palm, and squeeze with even pressure. Don't pump your hands up and down and don't sandwich the other person's hand between both of yours. Your grip should be firm but not bone crushing—you don't want to create the impression that you're attempting to overpower the other person. Likewise, a limp handshake sends a message of disinterest, possibly even disdain for the other person.

✔Treat men and women equally when shaking hands. It is as appropriate for a woman to offer her hand first as it is for a man. Similarly, in most business settings, a handshake is the customary greeting between women.

A true grip that projects self-confidence can help you create a favorable impression in any number of personal and professional situations. It is proper to extend a hand when
- meeting someone for the first time;
- greeting someone you haven't seen for awhile;
- saying hello to the host or hostess of an event;
- welcoming guests if you are the host or hostess; and
- saying your good-byes when leaving a gathering.

SELLING YOURSELF

FIRST IMPRESSIONS ARE AN ESSENTIAL PART OF DOING BUSINESS, and for most of us, an everyday occurrence. A good opening act increases your chances for an encore. While it's not impossible to overcome a bad beginning, the best way to prevent one is to approach each new encounter with courage and confidence, knowing that you have the power to make an unforgettable first impression. The manner in which you present yourself during an initial meeting can bolster your image, enhance your credibility, and open doors for new relationships and opportunities.

Chapter 2

PERSONAL PRESENCE:
Cultivating Charisma

> *You have within you a unique gem*
> *which you can either hide, or polish*
> *and show to the world.*
> —Elaina Zuker
>   President, Success Strategies Inc.

> *There are two kinds of people in the*
> *world: those who come into a room and*
> *say, "Here I am!" and those who come*
> *in and say, "Ah, there you are!"*
> —Anonymous

IMAGE IS SO MUCH MORE THAN THE WAY YOU LOOK. It's the way you communicate, act, and react. It's about attitude and goals, about possessing a strong sense of self-esteem and exuding a confidence that earns you the respect and admiration of others. It's believing in your own personal power and being comfortable using it.

Most of all, image is a matter of perceptions—not just how others see you, but how you see yourself. People who

15

project an assertive, competent, positive image usually succeed because they've learned how to face the world head-on. They've developed their own unique style and way of relating to others. They're not afraid to stand out in a crowd. In fact, their personal presence is so powerful that something almost magical seems to happen when they walk into a room. They bring to each encounter that elusive quality called charisma.

THE GIFT OF CHARISMA

Charisma originates from the Greek word for *gift*. Today we use it to describe personal magnetism, that unmistakable star quality that captures people's imaginations and inspires loyalty and devotion. Joan of Arc had it. So did Franklin Delano Roosevelt. Elizabeth Taylor, Michael Jackson, and Barbra Streisand possess it. So do Cher and Bill Clinton. And, of course, there are the Kennedys, a family whose charisma is so legendary it seems to be a genetic trait passed from one generation to the next.

Charisma is a potent quality easily recognized. But when asked to describe what draws us to dynamic individuals, we're hard-pressed to pinpoint their appeal. Charisma is difficult to define because it's different things to different people, and because it encompasses so many characteristics. "It can mean personality, charm, magnetism, and even star quality," says psychologist Alan D. Entin. "But it boils down to the ability to appeal to—and win the confidence of—the people around you."

Lawrence D. Schwimmer, author of *Winning Your Next Promotion in One Year (or Less!)*, attempted to define charisma by asking a number of professionals this question, "What is there about certain managers that makes them charismatic?" Here's a sample of what they said:

- "She's a natural leader. She exudes so much confidence and ability that I'd follow her anywhere."
- "If you walked into a crowded room, within two minutes you would notice him."
- "I can feel his strength and dynamism."
- "She really cares about people and has high integrity."
- "His enthusiasm is contagious!"

DO YOU HAVE CHARISMA?

Charisma is always a popular topic when Joyce speaks to groups about developing a polished image. Often she asks her audience to test their charisma by taking the following quiz, which appeared in a *USA TODAY* article several years ago. The quiz was developed by consultant Doe Lang, who wrote the book *Charisma: What It Is and How To Get It*.

Do you have charisma? To find out, check the appropiate box.

	True	False
1. My friends always come to me with their problems.	❏	❏
2. I often worry about the impression I'm making.	❏	❏
3. I am able to put people at ease.	❏	❏

4. I find it hard to get excited about many of the things that excite people I know. ❏   ❏

5. I always find something to like about everyone I meet. ❏   ❏

6. My mind often wanders when people address me. ❏   ❏

7. People are amazed by the fact that I always seem to be in high spirits. ❏   ❏

8. I find that most people don't have much to say. ❏   ❏

9. Most of my friends would be shocked to discover that I have problems not unlike theirs. ❏   ❏

10. I dislike people who burden me with details of their lives. ❏   ❏

ANSWERS

The most charismatic people answer "true" to the odd-numbered questions and "false" to the even-numbered ones. Hence, a charismatic person is trusted by others (1); makes people feel relaxed (3); has the ability to hone in on a person's good qualities (5); and always manages to be in a good mood (7); despite having problems like everyone else (9).

A charismatic person, being self-confident, never worries about the impression made on others (2); doesn't dampen a person's enthusiasm (4); always pays attention when being addressed (6); never writes people off (8); and always lends an ear when someone wants to talk (10).

To rate as charismatic, you need a score of seven or higher.

CULTIVATE YOUR CHARISMA

Because charisma has a certain mystique, there is some disagreement over how one acquires it—or whether that's even possible. Some folks maintain charisma is pure chemistry. Like talent, or natural beauty, it's a gift bestowed upon you before you ever enter this world. If you're not born with charisma, forget it.

But that assessment is based more on gut reaction than scientific research. Robert Abelson, professor of psychology at Yale, calls charisma "one of those factors that has a whiff of magic about it. It has a reputation of being somehow mysterious and more chemistry than psychology—so people tend not to study it. And that just adds to its mystery."

Others take a more pragmatic approach. Author Lang is convinced that charisma can be learned. "You don't have to be rich and you don't have to be good-looking," says Lang. Or a political figure, or a movie star, or famous at all, for that matter, to possess a certain pizzazz.

Schwimmer concurs. "You don't have to be born with this special quality: Charisma can be cultivated. My experience in training and counseling over 25,000 business and professional people throughout the country has taught me that while some people are naturally charismatic, most of us can learn to act, look, and speak in ways that will cause others to perceive us as being charismatic." But charisma is more than actions, Schwimmer adds, "it's a blend of style and substance."

Charisma is such an elusive quality that even the experts haven't been able to quantify it exactly. Still, charismatic individuals clearly share behaviors and beliefs that are credited with giving them a powerful presence. To boost your charismatic appeal, put these principles into practice:

Accentuate the Positive

"Most of us are attracted to optimistic people," says psychologist Entin. "Nobody likes hanging around a character who's always depressed, so you're going to have to keep your unhappiness under wraps if you want to develop charisma."

If the thought of a perpetually sunny disposition puts you off, consider this: optimists earn more. A study of insurance agents found that those who remained optimistic in spite of rejection sold thirty-seven percent more policies than their pessimistic counterparts! Why? Agents who took rejection personally started to expect that customers would turn them down. So they stopped trying as hard, their confidence dropped, and they began to project a feeling of failure that turned off potential clients.

Hear a Higher Calling

While charismatic people typically are very successful individuals, their motivations are rarely self-serving. If anything, they're focused on helping others reach their goals.

Charismatic leaders seem to have the ability to hear a higher calling and a desire to make a difference in the quality of people's lives.

"You must care about other people and want to serve everyone fairly," says Schwimmer. "The people with whom I've worked who stand out in a crowd aren't 'what-do-I-get-out-of-it?' or 'win-at-any-cost' go-getters. They aren't self-serving opportunists, users, or back-stabbers."

Watch Your Language

Certain words and gestures are noticeably absent from a charismatic person's communication. Language influences not only our attitudes but the disposition of the people around us. Consider the impact, for example, when you change the words "I'll try" to "I will" and "someday" to "today." Try substituting "I have to" to "I want to," "problem" to "opportunity," and "difficult" to "challenging."

Likewise, your body language can say you're confident and upbeat or communicate discouragement and defeat. It's simply a matter of standing up straight rather than slumping. Similarly, good eye contact, a firm handshake, and a warm smile can go a long way toward creating a positive perception. The very act of smiling can change the way you feel. Studies show that smiling relaxes facial tension while producing subtle chemical changes within your body. Another effect of smiling: the inflection of your voice goes up, which makes you sound warmer and more approachable.

Step into the Spotlight

"It's next to impossible to be charismatic unless you're in the public eye," says Schwimmer. "You must be visible so people are aware of your talents."

21

Charismatic people are not afraid to take the risks that make them stand out in a crowd—whether that means accepting a new professional assignment, developing a reputation as a mover-and-shaker in the community, or simply being recognized as the person who wears funky glasses and always knows the latest jokes.

Developing a signature style makes you appealing because most people find originality intriguing. "The very fact that you're distinguishing yourself from others is part of their perception of you as important," says Schwimmer.

Open Up to Others

Charismatic people have a way of making "everyone around them feel important, even when they're the ones in the spotlight," says Arnold Lazarus, a Rutgers University psychologist.

They create this feeling in a number of ways, beginning with the ability to sincerely enjoy other people's company. They become wholly engaged and completely focused when they have conversations. And they're not afraid to open up to others, which is key to cultivating charisma, says Lang. Listen carefully to people, she advises, and reveal a bit of your personal side in conversation to encourage intimacy.

Joseph Kennedy, son of Robert Kennedy and now a congressman from Massachusetts, is masterful at connecting with people in this way, says author Susan RoAne. In her book *How To Work A Room*, RoAne describes watching Kennedy mingle at a foundation fund-raiser. "The way he worked the room is a lesson to us all," RoAne writes.

The featured speaker, Kennedy made a point of visiting each and every table and talking with everyone at the event. "He wasn't just 'pumping flesh,' " RoAne recalls. "He was *connecting* with each person. He smiled, he looked into their eyes, he exuded warmth, he *touched* people, he was funny. He had something to say to everyone and he listened when they talked, hearing what they said and responding appropriately. He laughed. When he talked to me, he wasn't looking somewhere over my shoulder to see who else was in the room. It's impossible to fake charisma. The interest, the warmth, the sparkle, and the humor have to be real or people know it—especially under the glare of the spotlight, where Kennedy lives."

Put On a Happy Face

Learning to laugh at life's ups and downs, particularly your own, is not only healthy but it has the uncanny capability to improve your image. "Humor goes a long way in projecting magnetism," says psychologist Lazarus. "All of us want to laugh and be entertained."

Humor has a way of bringing people together and building rapport. We especially appreciate the ability of leaders and famous people to acknowledge their own foibles and vulnerabilities. Properly used, self-deprecation can be a powerful tool for gaining support. The "joke's on me" technique has been used effectively by many public figures, among them President Kennedy. After his wife's smashing success during their 1961 visit to France, Kennedy reportedly told the press: "Let me introduce myself. I'm the man who accompanied Jackie Kennedy to Paris."

Exercise Enthusiasm

Charismatic individuals radiate a vitality and zest that just naturally makes others want to be in their company. They approach the people and projects in their life with an enthusiasm that helps them stay motivated, and pushing ahead with seemingly little effort.

"Enthusiasm is the key to winning," says entrepreneur Paula Smith, who began to appreciate the power of enthusiasm after observing successful people in action. "One of the things I noticed consistently was these people had a positive aura about them. They didn't look down or depressed, and they didn't cry and moan—no matter what their personal circumstances."

Smith began to emulate these characteristics and was converted. "Enthusiasm can be developed," she says, "but it takes commitment, energy, and a sense of responsibility. I had to become 'electric' myself before I could have that effect on others."

WHILE NO FOOLPROOF FORMULA FOR CHARISMA EXISTS, you can cultivate the attitudes, presence, and power that conjure up that magical magnetism. "The potential for charisma is in all of us," says Lang. "The key is expressing ourselves so it comes through."

Chapter 3

A TOUCH OF POLISH:
Contemporary Etiquette for the Professional

> *There is no accomplishment so easy to acquire as politeness and none more profitable.*
> —George Bernard Shaw

> *Good manners are made up of petty sacrifices.*
> —Ralph Waldo Emerson

MANNERS ARE INTEGRAL TO THE IMPRESSIONS WE MAKE. The ability to smoothly maneuver your way through any business or social setting empowers you with poise and a sense of confidence that is naturally projected to everyone. Whether you're taking a client to lunch, introducing acquaintances at a cocktail party, or exchanging business cards at a professional gathering, etiquette can give you an extra edge.

When we say etiquette, we're not suggesting that you should be bridled by arcane rituals or adopt a set of stuffy

Victorian mannerisms. Rather, we're talking about principles of conduct that can enhance professional relationships and help you establish the kinds of friendships that contribute to a sense of well being. Etiquette, in our view, is less about arbitrary rules than what author and consultant Susan RoAne calls "that wonderful combination of courtesy, caring, and common sense." RoAne goes even further to make a distinction between knowing the rules of etiquette and being a person of manners: "Some people follow every rule of etiquette, but have a manner that is rude and patronizing."

If you're inclined to dismiss etiquette as meaningless ritual, consider this scenario shared by Linda and Wayne Phillips in their book *The Concise Guide to Executive Etiquette.* A chief executive officer, seeking to fill a highly visible position in his company, had narrowed the field to two equally desirable applicants. In a quandary as to which to choose, he took each out to dinner. The successful candidate? The one who ate the artichoke with aplomb.

Observing the social graces expected among civilized company invariably works to your benefit. "Good manners really can be a matter of life or death in business," says etiquette expert Hilka Klinkenberg, "In a strong economy, mastering business etiquette will give you a greater slice of the pie. In a downturn, the way people are treated could be the deciding factor in a company's survival."

Klinkenberg characterizes etiquette as the "oil that greases the wheels of commerce and industry. By behaving in an acceptable manner, you don't put unnecessary obstacles in your way. Instead, you present an image of yourself and your organization as caring, canny, and sophisticated. And, when you are perceived that way because of your manners, people tend to assume you're smart about other aspects of business, too, and want to deal with you."

Business people spend a great deal of time cultivating clients, contacts, and relationships with people they cannot afford to offend. But all too often entrepreneurs, as well as professionals climbing the corporate ladder, discover that their business standing puts them in situations that their upbringing never prepared them for. A power lunch with the company president is no time to reveal you're a little rough around the edges.

"Good manners are one of the hallmarks of professional presence," says image consultant Bixler. "It is impossible to be considered sophisticated and competent without them. No matter what our background, whether our parents schooled us in etiquette or not, as professionals it is our obligation to fill in the blanks."

That's what we want to do here: provide you with a working knowledge of everyday etiquette that will put you at ease in most business and social settings. We also aim to help you appreciate how observing common courtesies can pay you back richly by encouraging positive responses in others. Starting in this chapter and continuing throughout the book, you'll find tips to give you "personal polish" and perfect your image as a competent, confident person.

GREAT BEGINNINGS

More and more busy professionals are finding that the lines between social and business activities are blending. Self-employed people especially find it hard to separate their work and personal lives—even if they want to. Witness the woman who, having started a yacht-rental business, told a reporter with *The Wall Street Journal*, "I can never seem to get away. Every time I go to a party, I am thinking of selling the service."

Rather than complaining, this woman could be putting her passion for her business to work in social situations, says author and consultant RoAne. "In today's business environment, you need to be comfortable in social and quasi-social situations where you can make contact with potential customers, as well as other people who can help your business succeed."

For many people, such encounters are anything but enjoyable. In fact, when asked to rate situations that make them most uncomfortable, *USA TODAY* readers put attending an event with strangers at the top of the list. "I think most people are basically shy," observes Joyce. "And if you can remember that, it makes it so much easier to be the first one to offer your hand."

Mingling with Ease

Since interacting with new people and facing unfamiliar situations is an everyday occurrence in many professions, most of us have no choice but to overcome, or at least ignore, our insecurities if we want to be successful. "Going out is the first step to creating visibility," says RoAne. "We cannot create a positive presence unless we are present." An expert on savvy socializing, she cites ten characteristics of "magnificent minglers." They

1. are able to make others feel comfortable.
2. appear to be confident and at ease.
3. can laugh at themselves (not at others).
4. show interest in others: they maintain eye contact, self-disclose, ask questions, and actively listen.

5. extend themselves to others: they lean into a greeting with a firm handshake and a smile.
6. convey a sense of energy and enthusiasm— a joie de vivre.
7. are well-rounded, well-informed, well-intentioned, and well-mannered.
8. know vignettes or stories of actual events that are interesting, humorous, and appropriate.
9. introduce people to each other with an infectious enthusiasm (there is no other kind) that motivates conversation.
10. convey respect and genuinely like people— the core of communication.

Though momentary panic before stepping into a new situation is quite natural, here are two ways you can increase your comfort level:

Know what to expect. Before the event, call your host to discuss details such as who will be attending and any special instructions about attire or time that you need to know. If it's a professional or business event, you should also ask about the agenda and any special activities.

Set your own agenda. One of the best ways to prevent a feeling of aimlessness, which simply fuels your anxiety, is to decide what you want to accomplish during the gathering. For instance, your goal may be to get better acquainted with coworkers or fellow professionals; or to meet prospective clients; or to connect with someone who has expertise you need. Whatever your agenda, try to find out in advance who'll be attending the gathering. This information can help focus your energies so you reap the most benefits from your attendance.

Opening Lines: The Art Of Small Talk

One of the hardest parts about walking into a room full of strangers is knowing we're going to have to strike up a conversation with one of them. "Most of us face situations—whether it's at a cocktail party or in the hall waiting for the elevator—where the capacity for small talk is all important," says *Working Woman* editor Adele Scheele. "And almost everybody has, at one time or another, failed at chitchatting."

Even if you're not the type who rattles off witty one-liners or always has an amusing anecdote ready, you don't have to resign yourself to the role of social wallflower. Anyone can learn the gift of gab—all it takes is a little practice and a few tips from seasoned experts.

"The key to chatting successfully with strangers lies in a provocative opening," advises Scheele. "If you see someone wearing a pin, tie, ring, or brooch, ask if there's a story behind it. At a Christmas party, ask the important-looking stranger at the bar to name the best Christmas party she ever attended. Such questions are almost guaranteed to get the conversation going.

"And the questions don't have to be brilliant, either", adds Scheele. "Everyone likes to tell his or her stories; people are usually so flattered that they won't even notice if a question isn't the smartest or smoothest."

You also might want to experiment with Eleanor Roosevelt's approach to small talk: She reportedly ran through the alphabet looking for topics that sparked interest. For instance, she might start with apple pies and move to baseball and so on until she found something that clicked with the person she was speaking to.

And RoAne, in her book *How To Work A Room,* says, "You will walk into a room with more confidence if you have at least three pieces of small talk prepared—light conversations you can have with anyone you meet."

That technique has certainly worked for Andrea Nierenberg, president of Sales Boosters, a training and consulting firm. A masterful networker, Nierenberg keeps a "small-talk notebook," a daily diary in which she records her thoughts, observations about her experiences, and interesting bits of news she might read or hear. "Today, for example," she explains, "in *The Wall Street Journal* there was an article about the ongoing war between two major computer companies. I clipped the article for a speech I'm working on, but I also entered it in my small-talk notebook because I could be at a party this week where it would be a good piece of information to open a conversation." Before any kind of social or professional gathering, Nierenberg thumbs through her notebook, looking for anecdotes and tidbits she can use to break the ice when meeting new people.

But what if you're so painfully shy you can't even imagine striking up a conversation with someone you don't know? No problem, says Nierenberg, who suggests this simple but fail-safe technique for mastering small talk: Smile, look the other person in the eye, and ask a question.

"You can come across as the most charming person if you have great eye contact—if you really look people in the eye—which is something most shy people are afraid to do," counsels Nierenberg.

As for conversation openers, nothing beats a question. "Even if you're *truly shy,* what's the easiest thing in the world to do? Ask someone a question. Not a yes-no question," Nierenberg explains, "but an open-ended question that gets the other person talking. When you do this, a funny thing happens—the other person starts to do all the work. So it takes the pressure off you. Then, all you have to do to keep the conversation going is say things like 'that's interesting' or 'tell me more.' "

At first, most people don't buy this simple small-talk technique, which Nierenberg routinely teaches at her training sessions. Shy people especially doubt it because they're convinced they could never master the art of schmoozing. So Nierenberg urges them on with one more tip: "Act as if."

In other words, if you want to be a great schmoozer, she explains, just act like you already are one. "Project in your mind how you want to be, then go out and schmooze with somebody. It doesn't matter who—it can be the guy in the grocery store who's buying fruit. Look him in the eye, smile, and ask a question. I promise you, it works every time—like a charm," Nierenberg confides. "But I can't tell you how many people have come back to me, saying, 'I can't believe it—it really worked.' "

The Name Game

Many people panic at the prospect of having to make an introduction. They're not sure about who to introduce to whom, or how to handle titles. Worst of all, what if they can't remember someone's name?

Relax. If you concentrate on being personable and gracious, chances are you won't do anything unforgivable. The most important thing to remember about an introduction, says Letitia Baldridge in her *Complete Guide to Executive Manners,* is to "do it, even if you forget names, get confused, or blank out on the proper procedure. Introducing people is one of the most important acts of business life..."

Baldridge boils down the intricacies of introductions to one simple rule that will suffice in most situations: introduce the "less important" person to the "more important" person. For example, introduce a

- younger person to an older person.
- peer in your company to a peer in another company.
- nonofficial person to an official person.
- junior executive to a senior executive.
- fellow executive to a customer or client.

As for using titles, she says, "When introducing people of equal standing, you do not have to use a title unless you are introducing an older person, a professional, or someone with official rank." For example, you might use a title when introducing a doctor, or a politician, or a member of the clergy—but not if you're talking to two executives.

When making introductions, it's nice to offer a brief point of reference that may help the new acquaintances connect. For example, say something such as, "Tom Jacobs, I'd like you to meet Joe Taylor. We worked together at Company XYZ." As they shake hands, you might add, "Joe, like you, Tom is an avid baseball fan."

Other introduction pointers:

✔ A man is generally always introduced to a woman, with one possible exception: If there's a notable difference in their rank—for instance, if he's president of the company and she's an assistant supervisor in the same firm—keep in mind Baldridge's simple rule about less important to more important.

✔ When introducing your spouse, especially in professional or quasi-social settings, say, "This is Mary, my wife," not "This is my wife Mary." Why? Because when you describe your relationship first, it demeans your spouse and implies— though this may not be your intent—that the person belongs to you. Offering the name first suggests your spouse is an independent person, who just happens to be married to you.

✔ If you forget someone's name, most experts agree it's best to be honest. You might say, "I'm having a hard time with names today, why don't you introduce yourselves." (Likewise, if you sense someone is having trouble recalling your name, graciously come to their rescue by saying something like, "Hi, I'm Kathy, and we met at the Orlando conference.")

Card Tricks

It pays to carry your business card with you at all times because social situations often present excellent opportunities to make professional contacts. Joyce makes it a practice to always tuck a few into a pocket because "it's undesirable to be digging around in a purse or briefcase." Other people prefer to use a case specifically designed for this purpose; business card cases come in a variety of styles and usually can be purchased at office supply stores. Or, you may find it useful to devise your own system. "I use a large cigarette case, with a baseball card to divide my cards from those I've collected," says RoAne.

The etiquette of presenting your business card is largely governed by common sense:

- Never present a card that is out of date, soiled, or dog-eared.
- Be selective about handing out your card. Never force it on anyone, especially someone in a more senior position.
- When calling on someone new, such as a client, present your card when you shake hands. This prevents any confusion or embarrassment if they don't know or can't remember your name. However, if you are meeting with people you don't know, it's best to wait for someone else to encourage the exchange. (Unless, of course, you are the most senior person in the room.)
- Depending on the nature of your business, you may want to include your home phone on the card. If you do this, it's best to have a dedicated phone line, or else train everyone in your household to answer in the proper manner.

Personal Polish Tip

When someone hands you a business card, read it carefully, make a complimentary comment about it, and most importantly, hold it as you talk. Keeping the card in hand, instead of immediately putting it away, is a nonverbal sign of respect. It also can be useful in helping you remember the person's name.

MIXING BUSINESS WITH PLEASURE

Social settings often offer great opportunities to connect with people you might not otherwise meet but who could play an important role in your professional future. While some etiquette experts take a hard line on mixing business with pleasure, in our experience, it's foolish not to take advantage of such situations. But it pays to understand the consequences and nuances involved—because there's a fine line between making a connection and becoming a social boor.

Say you meet someone at a party who seems genuinely interested in your work. There's nothing wrong with answering a few questions about your business or job, or trading professional tips, or discussing collcagues or clients you have in common. But keep the conversation light and don't let it monopolize your time or attention. Most hosts and hostesses don't appreciate having their dinner party, birthday celebration, or child's wedding turned into an impromptu business meeting. The other risk of becoming immersed in a heavy duty conversation is that you miss out on the chance to mingle and may even alienate other guests who regard such behavior as rude.

If you find yourself cornered into talking business at a gathering that's clearly social, try to gracefully change the subject. If the person persists, simply hand him or her your business card and say, "Let's not talk business now; may I call you next week?"

Personal Polish Tip

Thank the host or hostess before you leave any event. Even if you're at a professional gathering, such as a trade association luncheon, someone has spent time planning the food, the program, and countless other details required to organize the event. If at all possible, seek that person out and graciously acknowledge their efforts and hospitality.

HIGH-TECH ETIQUETTE

Cellular phones, computerized calendars and address books, fax machines, voice mail, electronic mail…it seems there's no end to the gimmicks, gadgets, and gizmos being created to help professionals on the go work anywhere, anytime. And they do, often with little appreciation for how this around-the-clock accessibility can quickly cross the line between convenient communication and unwelcome intrusions.

"While the new electronic office is a bright pasture of opportunity, it's also filled with etiquette time bombs that can go off in your face and make you look like a jerk," writes business executive Gil Schwartz in an article for *Working Woman* magazine. "Being a jerk in the nineties is just as undesirable as it was in the eighties and possibly even in the seventies."

Modern technology can be addictive, so much so that it's easy to lose sight of even the most basic dictums of decorum. People who would never dream of being inconsiderate or rude in person commit embarrassing blunders, thanks to technology. One legendary example is the E-mail escapade of journalist Linda Ellerbee. As the story goes, early in her career, while working for Associated Press, Ellerbee wrote an unflattering description of her boss in a message she sent to a friend via the company's electronic mail system. But an accidental key stroke saved the presumably privileged missive and programmed it to go across the news wires. The next morning, during a routine transmission, Ellerbee's note went racing over the wires to AP offices in four states. And her job went out the window.

While Ellerbee's electronic escapade is legendary, high-tech faux pas are more common than you might imagine. "I've been told many horror stories by people who attended plays and operas and dined in better restaurants only to have the event interrupted by beepers, portable phones, and watch alarms," says RoAne. Here's one such story, which she shares in her latest book, *The Secrets of Savvy Networking:*

> A keynote speaker was addressing an audience of three hundred interior designers when in midsentence she heard a phone ring loudly. Knowing everyone else heard the ringing, she responded by saying "If a phone did not ring, then I just learned I have tinnitus." The audience laughed, and the speaker asked the phone-carrier to stand and introduce himself, as he already had the floor. "I made a judgment call, but all I could think of was how someone could be (a) so misguided in their self-importance and (b) so rude," shared the stunned presenter whose humor saved the speech.

Bad manners and modern technology don't automatically go hand in hand. It's possible to take advantage of the convenience and time savings these high-tech inventions offer, without becoming an insensitive boor, if you follow a few common sense rules.

Fax Faux Pas

Failure to appreciate the public nature of fax technology accounts for most blunders. In office settings, particularly, machines are often shared by several people. So gauge your transmissions accordingly. For instance, don't send confidential or sensitive information, such as your résumé, unless you really intend to put out the word that you're job hunting.

The first rule of faxing is to be considerate of the faxee. You can avoid fax abuse by keeping in mind:

• Unsolicited material is rarely welcome.

• Cartoons, jokes, and cute messages are regarded as unprofessional in many offices. (Such transmissions are best reserved for people with whom you've already established a relationship and mutually agreed to use your fax machines as an informal mode for staying in touch.)

• A fax always should be accompanied by a cover note that states who it's to, who it's from, the date, and number of pages. You may even want to include a place for the time as well—especially if the nature of your business means you will be sending more than one fax to the same person in the same day. Putting the time on your cover sheet also is a plus if a thermal fax is to be distributed to several people, since this information is typically cut off during photocopying.

- Lengthy faxes—anything more than two pages— should be cleared before transmission to make sure the faxee can afford to have his or her machine tied up for several minutes and that what you're sending is deemed urgent enough to warrant a fax. (Entrepreneurs who monitor their costs closely are careful not to waste fax paper on materials that could be mailed just as easily.) Also, most hotels charge not only for sending but receiving faxes. So be considerate of your recipient; if you must send a traveling professional information by fax, economize on words to keep their costs down.

Personal Polish Tip

Follow up a fax with a phone call. More often than not, this is simply a nice gesture. But it can be a business lifesaver: In our experience, there's a "Fax Never-Never Land" where transmissions mysteriously disappear to, usually with no warning on your end that something extraordinary has happened!

E-Mail Manners

Electronic mail offers the obvious advantage of allowing correspondence to be shared at any time that's convenient to the sender and receiver. The disadvantage is that, unlike traditional mail, your memos and messages are potentially accessible to anyone on the system.

Some E-mail pointers:
1. Follow the same rules you would use for traditional written correspondence. Pay attention to
   spelling, grammar, and punctuation, and be sure
   to give your memos a heading and a signature.

2. Be mindful of your tone and message. As a general rule, don't use E-mail for any information
   that you wouldn't want to risk being retrieved
   and read by anyone on the system.

3. Don't abuse the system by sending "junk mail."
   Workers in corporations commonly complain
   that they are bombarded with messages from
   strangers. It's unprofessional and inconsiderate
   to treat an E-mail system set up for business like
   a community bulletin board for advertising or
   selling used merchandise or tickets to sports
   events.

Telephone Techniques

Though telephones have been part of our daily lives for a
long time, the potential for abuse arises every time a new
feature hits the market. Take, for instance, call waiting. It's
hard to know which is more frustrating—hearing a busy
signal or reaching your party only to be put on hold while
he or she decides which of the two incoming calls is most
important. Similarly, speakerphones sound like a great
idea, but many callers find their echo quality infuriating.

Our purpose here is not to critique current telephone
technology, but simply to point out that these new inventions demand increased sensitivity to basic manners. Often,

a phone call is your first and only chance to impress the person on the other end of the line. At that moment, neither the equipment you're using nor even the topic of your conversation has the power to say as much about you as the manner in which you handle the call.

With that in mind, here are some tips on telephone manners that will serve you well, regardless of where you stand with today's technology.

Listen to yourself. "The voice you use should be professional, clear, and resonant enough that people listen to what you have to say," advises Eileen Sinett, a communications executive skilled in voice training. "If you have poor pitch, low or loud volume, or a raspy or nasal quality to your voice, you often don't get your message across. People react to how your voice sounds and never get to what you're saying."

To create a positive telephone personality, your voice should be direct, unhurried, confident, and upbeat. You may want to try a technique used by announcers: smile when you're talking. That smile can be "heard" and your voice just naturally becomes brighter and more pleasant. Sit up straight when answering the phone—it makes your voice sound alert. Also, a greeting, such as "good morning," gives callers the impression you're glad they called. Then listen actively. Periodic responses such as "yes," "I understand," and "certainly," let the person on the other end of the line know you're interested in the conversation.

Always identify yourself when placing a call. This is a good practice, no matter how many times you've spoken in the past—because a busy professional engages in dozens of conversations during the course of a day. Expecting someone to instantly recognize your voice, or putting them in a position to have to guess who you are, is neither realistic nor businesslike. Get your conversation off to a good start by identifying yourself immediately and succinctly stating the reason for your call. As a matter of courtesy, it's also a good idea to inquire whether this a convenient time to talk, especially if you anticipate your conversation will take awhile.

Make technology work for you, not against you. We urge you to resist the temptation to treat answering machines and voice mail as auditions. Theatrics, special sound effects, jokes, and overly clever messages are rarely effective and should be avoided in professional situations.

When recording the greeting for your answering machine or voice mail, focus on being concise and providing only the most necessary information: your name and any instructions the caller needs to leave a message. It's also helpful to let callers know when they can expect a return call, either from you personally or a coworker.

Likewise, when reaching someone else's answering device, be sure to state your name, the reason for your call, the best time to return your call, and your phone number. If possible, try to minimize the need for a return call. Two common message mistakes: first, forgetting to include the area code with your phone number, and second, assuming that if you've talked before, the recipient will automatically know your number. Including your phone number, especially when calling people who are traveling, may make the

Personal Polish Tip

Call yourself from time to time. It's easy to record a message and forget about it, so get into the habit of periodically calling your own number to check the impression you're sending out. Is your message still timely? Does it provide the necessary information for callers? Is the voice quality fine? Do callers have sufficient time to leave a message?

difference between having your call returned immediately or being forced to wait until they return and can retrieve your number from their records.

Return your calls. With the advent of answering machines and voice mail, it seems some folks have vowed to never pick up a receiver. In fact, we've heard of people so adept at high-tech telephone tag that they talk only to machines, avoiding person-to-person conversations altogether.

While the new technology clearly can be a useful tool in as much as it enables you to manage your time by screening calls, we don't advocate it as an excuse for bad manners. Granted, receiving unsolicited messages on your machine and being expected to respond can be annoying. But refuse to do so, and you run the risk of earning a reputation for being rude. More importantly, you may be missing an unexpected opportunity. If you're an entrepreneur, you simply can't afford not to return calls—even from strangers.

For example, once, while on a business trip, Joyce received a message from a large business services company. Her first thought was, "Great, they probably want to sell us a photocopy machine." Still, as is her practice, she returned the call, only to learn it had come from the director of corporate communications, who wanted Joyce to work with the president of the company. The moral of the story: It doesn't pay to pre-judge the worth of any message—even when it's from someone you've never met—because, as Joyce says, "All my clients are strangers, until I work with them."

GESTURES OF GRATITUDE AND GENEROSITY

The human touch is often missing in today's high-tech world. So when someone takes the time to personally show that he or she cares, the gesture generally makes a posi-tive—and lasting—impression.

The Written Word

Even if manners weren't emphasized in your upbringing, most of us learned as children that it's rude not to send thank-you notes for gifts and that formal invitations require a reply. Thus, our goal here is not to recap the dic-tates of basic letter-writing etiquette, but to emphasize that there are times when a note isn't necessary—but it sure is nice. Recognizing and responding to those moments with a sincere, personal, well-written note is a gracious, thoughtful gesture that can go a long way toward building relationships.

"Powerful people get that way by paying attention to details like writing notes," says etiquette expert Hilka Klinkenberg. "Lyndon Johnson wrote to everybody he met so that, no matter what you thought of him, you felt good getting a personal note from the president of the United States."

Handwritten letters are appropriate for conveying congratulations, appreciation, apologies, and condolences.

Some noteworthy situations:
- ✔ A colleague experiences a celebratory life change, such as getting married or the birth of a child.
- ✔ An acquaintance earns special recognition, such as winning an award or being asked to speak at an event.
- ✔ A busy professional agrees to meet with you or offers to put you in touch with someone whose help you need.
- ✔ A supplier with whom you regularly do business rushes an order for supplies, enabling you to complete a project on tight deadline.

Handwritten notes also are proper when you want to extend an informal invitation. Likewise, it's nice but not necessary to send a note to the host or hostess after attending a dinner or cocktail party. Your notes need not be long to have an impact. Nor should they be overly effusive. To illustrate what we mean, here are three samples from the National Institute of Business Management's book, *Mastering Business Style*.

Dear George,
So glad to hear about your promotion. It's always a
pleasure to hear good news about someone you know
and admire. Congratulations and best wishes.

Sincerely,

Dear Fred,
Congratulations on (your birthday, the birth of your
child, your anniversary, etc.). It's always a pleasure to
write about happy events in the lives of (friends, asso-
ciates, colleagues, etc.). Best wishes.

Sincerely,

Dear Mary,
I want you to know how much I appreciated your fine
hospitality during my visit to your home. The cocktail
party on Saturday was a delight and I enjoyed meeting
Bob and Janice. Indeed, you are lucky to have them as
close friends. Thank you so much for a wonderful three days.

Sincerely,

While any of these messages could have been conveyed
with a phone call, there are definite advantages to penning
a note. Once you develop the habit, writing a note only
takes a moment and it's a convenient way to stay in touch.
Unlike a phone call, which has the potential to disrupt the
recipient's day, a letter can be enjoyed at leisure.

More importantly, a personal note has a lasting quality. A
handwritten thank-you, for example, "is tangible evidence
of good work that can be shown to one's boss, copied, and

circulated to the entire department, placed in one's scrap book or portfolio, reread and enjoyed at one's leisure," observe the Phillips in their book *The Concise Guide to Executive Etiquette.* "The note becomes a continual reminder of what a pleasure it is to do business with a person who cares."

One of the best thank-you notes Joyce ever received was written on an airline's sick bag. Her client, who traveled a lot, was so impressed with Joyce's services that he didn't want to wait until he returned home to write and let her know. So he took advantage of the only paper handy on the plane—the air sick bag tucked in his seat pocket. "I couldn't believe it," Joyce recalls. "I was so touched I framed it, and the note now hangs in my office."

Personal Polish Tip

Keep small, plain thank-you notes handy on your desk. Or tuck a few in your date book or briefcase for when you're traveling or have time between appointments. Every week, make a point of sending one note to a colleague, customer, or vendor. This simple gesture, which only takes a moment, will be long remembered because so few people do it.

Giving Gifts

Sometimes a simple thank-you won't do—a grander gesture is in order. Gifts have the power to communicate many messages: "You are important to me," or "Good luck on your new venture," or "I remember your special day." The selection and presentation of a gift, especially in professional arenas, must be handled with care because gift-giving says a lot about you, your company, and how you do business. Gifts are "a form of communication and a marketing tool—like a memo or presentation," says Dawn Bryan, consultant and author of *The Art and Etiquette of Gift Giving*.

A business gift list typically includes customers and clients, employees, and potential prospects for business. The most popular gift-giving occasion is Christmas, according to *Incentive,* a New York–based magazine that polls hundreds of executives each year on their business gift-giving habits. Other common gift-giving occasions include plant visits, trade shows, seminars, sales calls, company outings and meetings, birthdays and anniversaries.

Creating your own gift-giving occasions is even better, because it conveys that you're not only caring, but original. Bryan offers these examples: an Irish importer who sends shamrock plants to customers on St. Patrick's Day; a New York law firm that shakes its staid image each Valentine's Day by giving chocolate hearts to its support staff; and an entrepreneur who sends flowers to female colleagues for International Women's Day.

Unexpected attention—a gift "just because"—can be a truly delightful experience. Say, for instance, a client is opening a new branch office and you want to wish the operation a success. Or you want to recognize a colleague who's earned an honorary degree or congratulate a coworker for winning a new account.

Observing such milestones with flowers or a clever token can build goodwill and strengthen your relationship with the recipient. Or ruin it, if your generosity is misinterpreted as ostentatious, or worse, a bribe. Impulse gift-giving requires judgment, warns etiquette expert Baldridge. A gift must have a "natural, proper reason" or it will be received with suspicion, she says in her *Complete Guide to Executive Manners*.

That's why entrepreneur Jean Gardner doesn't give gifts to people with whom she's currently negotiating business. "I might invite the potential client to a meal during the holidays instead of giving a gift," she explains. "Later, I could give them a gift to mark the signing of the contract."

Thus, the two most important considerations in business gift-giving are your relationship with the recipient and the appropriateness of the occasion. This is especially true if you do business with people from countries or cultures that are foreign to you. Well-intentioned though your gesture may be, sending "Merry Christmas" cards to people who don't celebrate the holiday is insensitive and may earn you the reputation for being narrow-minded—or even cost you future business. Likewise, it's not wise to send wine or liquor to someone whose religion forbids the use of alcohol or to someone who's a member of Alcoholics Anonymous.

There's definitely an art to business gift-giving, say the experts, who offer these pointers.

Think About the Recipient

Do you know anything about the person's hobbies, habits, or enthusiasms? The more individual you can make a gift, the greater your chances of success. If you know a person is an avid collector of, say, antique toys or teapots, it's perfectly appropriate to add to his or her collection. Another idea that Joyce has found goes over especially well with busy clients who travel a lot: gift certificates for massages and facials, or "pamper-me" personalized gift baskets.

Conversely, if you're not personally close to the recipient, opt for a gift that is practical and preferably "gender-free." Examples of such gifts include business card cases, calendars, memo-pad holders, pens, letter openers, picture frames, and small electronic gadgets. But even then, give some thought to matching your selection to the recipient— don't buy dozens of the same item to distribute to every client and colleague on your gift list.

Joyce likes to buy her holiday gifts during the summer at craft fairs or when she travels on business. One year, for example, she purchased hand-blown glass paperweights for all her clients and professional friends. But she made the gifts personal by choosing each paperweight with a particular client in mind. "People were really very touched," she recalls, "and said things like, 'How did you know I just redid my living room in those colors?' "

Insist on Quality

A gift need not be expensive, but even a small token should be tasteful and high in quality. Remember, your selection is a reflection of you and your company. In particular, logo gifts should be given with care. Poorly made merchandise or gadgets that are good for little more than collecting dust will come across not as gifts, but as a cheap advertising gimmick.

Give of Yourself

There's nothing wrong with using a gift to help build your image, if the selection communicates something meaningful about who you are. For example, one Michigan-based manufacturer sends customers baskets of made-in-Michigan food products at Christmas. Similarly, a Louisiana company sends Mardi Gras treats to out-of-town clients each January.

Say you want to convey a sense that your business is on the cutting edge, then high-tech gadgets might be appropriate. Or if health or the environment tie in with your products or services, you might consider gifts of sports, or outdoor equipment, or even books on the subject. For example, we recently heard about "Gift of a Tree" certificates that offer recipients a choice of either having a tree planted in their name in the ancient Lancandon Mayan Rain Forest or receiving a starter kit with step-by-step instructions for growing a tree themselves.

Get Professional Help When in Doubt

If you're really in a gift-giving dilemma, either because you're short on time or lack confidence in your creativity, consider using experts. Nearly two-thirds of the people who buy business gifts use gift services or consultants, according to one study.

Consultants offer services such as developing gift and incentive programs, maintaining gift-giving records, arranging for personalization of gifts, and wrapping and shipping. Similarly, many major department stores, specialty retailers, and even some museum gift shops have corporate gift-giving divisions or personal shoppers to assist you in making professionally proper selections. One word of advice: When seeking gift-buying advice, deal with reputable professionals who come to you through referrals or who work at well-known establishments, such as Tiffany's, or major department stores in your area.

Bottom line, if you're new to business gift-giving, rely on your instincts. "Give gifts only if you feel comfortable doing so," advises Bryan. "If not, your discomfort will show, and the gift will come across as stilted. What makes a business gift—or any gift—effective is the thought and feeling behind it."

THE RULES OF ETIQUETTE ARE CONSTANTLY EVOLVING and the ideas presented here are by no means an exhaustive review of modern manners. Many volumes have been written on this timely topic, so if you need greater guidance, start at the shelves of your local bookstore or library. You also may want to confer with colleagues at work or in your professional networks. In our experience, most people appreciate it when someone makes the effort to understand what's appropriate behavior. So if you're confronted with a situation where you really don't know what's proper, just ask. Rather than being put off, your companions most likely will be charmed that you cared enough to mind your manners.

Worrying about minor manner mishaps or how you'll be perceived prevents you from making meaningful connections in your life. But, as we've said, knowing the precise rule at a particular time is not nearly as important as developing an awareness of your surroundings and a sensitivity to the people in it. If you make an effort to be polite, approachable, and show respect for the person with whom you're dealing, we can almost guarantee that, whatever the circumstances, your conduct will be proper.

PART TWO

Selling Yourself

Chapter 4

THE POWER OF PERSUASION:
Interpersonal Communication Skills

> *The greatest illusion about communication is the belief that it has been accomplished.*
> —George Bernard Shaw

> *The most important single ingredient in the formula of success is knowing how to get along with people.*
> —Theodore Roosevelt

WE ALL KNOW HOW TO CARRY ON A CONVERSATION. You talk. Someone listens. Then the other person makes a comment while you listen. Back and forth, back and forth, the conversation bounces between speakers.

You're both talking, but are you really communicating? Now that's another matter altogether. Most of us have experienced breakdowns in communication—moments when our words and actions didn't jibe with our intentions. Or, we discovered too late that what we thought we heard wasn't what the other person really meant, or, the conversation becomes so heated that we fail to manage our mouths, and suddenly we're saying things we instantly want to take back.

Although most people acknowledge the importance of good communication—the art of conversing, listening, negotiating, and compromising that routinely guides us through life—few of us do it as well as we would like. Messages get garbled and sometimes our efforts to communicate create more problems than they solve. Worse yet, we make the mistake of underestimating the power communication exerts on our success, every day, in ways big and small. Consider these findings:

- Research conducted by the Carnegie Institute of Technology, and confirmed by other studies, shows that about 15 percent of financial and career success is attributable to technical skills, while 85 percent is attributable to interpersonal or "people skills"—the ability to interact with others.

- Human resources professionals estimate that more than 80 percent of the people who fail at their jobs do so for one reason: they don't relate well to other people.

Not surprisingly, communication is a hot topic in the business community. A great deal of management time and training is spent on communication, in an effort to help employees appreciate the value of productive professional relationships. In fact, it's hard to imagine a situation, professionally or personally, that doesn't depend on communication—and many of our problems can be linked to the lack of it. Knowing how to express ourselves so we deal effectively with others has a direct impact on our ability to move ahead in life. Despite talent or ambition, dreams or determination, almost everything we accomplish is ultimately done through the cooperation and support of others.

Experts characterize our interpersonal communication style as an "inescapable calling card" that immediately announces to the world who we are, how we feel, and what we expect from ourselves and others. The ability to convey your ideas effectively can help you, for example, gain approval for a new project, cement a business relationship, convince a prospective employer you're the best candidate, or simply persuade someone to give you a helping hand during a hectic day. Likewise, ignoring how you do—and don't—communicate can thwart your best efforts and leave you wondering why you're so often misunderstood, or why you can't get the support you need to move ahead, whatever your goals.

Mastering effective interpersonal communication is such a wide-ranging and complex topic that whole books have been written on single skills, such as listening or negotiating. In this chapter, we'll touch on some of the most common communication shortcomings, with the intent of making you more aware of how your interpersonal style can help, or hinder, your success. Drawing from an assortment of experts, we'll share nuts-and-bolts techniques and tips, plus tests to help you identify areas you need to brush up on. Building on this foundation, we'll continue our discussion in chapter 5 by exploring the dynamics of selling, a skill that depends heavily on interpersonal communication.

PUT YOUR COMMUNICATION STYLE TO THE TEST

Anyone who wants to get ahead, especially in today's competitive economic environment, must develop a diverse set of communication skills. Equally important, you must be interpersonally savvy—you must recognize, depending on the situation and the individuals involved, what communication skills are most likely to help you achieve mutually beneficial results. Sometimes you may need to speak up for yourself, even protest a turn of events. Other times, the wisest step you can take is to keep quiet and listen to others' ideas. Clearly, there are no pat approaches when you're dealing with people.

To help give you a feel for the broad-reaching topic of interpersonal communications, we want to share this quiz created by the editors of *Communication Briefings,* a professional newsletter. This quick test broaches many of the techniques we'll be covering, and going over the questions will start you thinking about how your own communication style measures up.

1. Do I usually try to see the other person's point of view, even if I disagree?
2. Do I ever ask others for feedback on my communication style?
3. Do I know what my image is among my co-workers—or am I assuming I know what it is?
4. Do I resent the good ideas of others? Am I envious of others' successes? (Be totally honest with yourself.)
5. Do I often start communicating with a chip on my shoulder? Am I looking for confrontation,

especially from people on my staff and those
who provide services for me?
6. Am I insensitive to criticism? Do I block it from
coming in by sending signals that it is unwelcome? Do I defend against it as soon as it arrives?
7. Have I looked at all the ways I communicate—
orally, in writing, through dress, through office
arrangement, through body expressions. Have I
ever asked another person to help me look at
the ways?

People skills are unquestionably among the most important skills you can possess. In the following sections, we'll
explore communication techniques that can help you work
more productively with your boss and colleagues, establish
better relationships with clients and customers, and even
improve interactions with the important people in your
personal life.

Talking Doesn't Equal Communication

Communication doesn't mean filling every possible
moment with speech—sometimes silence says more than
words ever could. Yet the ability to listen, to really hear
what others are saying, is one of the most underrated communication skills.

"In our society, we simply do not know how to listen, we
place little value on listening, and there is little information
available on the topic," say Richard Weaver and Curt
Bechler, authors of the book *Listen to Win* (MasterMedia,
1993). "Listening effectively is a skill that applies no matter
who you are, what you are, or where you are."

You can't hope to succeed, especially in selling situations such as a job interview, if you don't make the effort to understand what the other person needs, wants, and expects. One study, in fact, showed that good listeners are promoted more often than those with less-effective listening skills.

Listening means giving yourself time to absorb what's being said. Good listeners appreciate the power of silence and they've trained themselves to be comfortable with the pauses and wordless moments that occur naturally in conversations. As Charles DeGaulle once observed, "Silence is the ultimate weapon of power." By learning to use silence to your advantage, you not only can make people feel like they've been heard, you stand a better chance of getting them to truly listen to you.

So You Think You Listen?

Listening well is an art, and no one is good at it all the time. Worse yet, we make the mistake of thinking we don't have to work at it. "That's because many people believe listening is a natural skill, something we're born with," says Stephen N. Anderson, vice president of quality management and communications for Westmoreland Coal Company.

Instead of being natural listeners, though, many of us develop skills that condition us to not listen, to actually block out what someone else is saying. By overlooking these "non-listening skills," we easily can miss important messages. To assess your listening skills, Anderson offers the following test.

Respond to each statement with one of these answers.
1–always; 2–usually; 3–sometimes; 4–almost never:

1. I listen for facts rather than ideas. _____

2. I mentally prepare what I want to say in
    response while the person is still talking. _____

3. I pretend to understand when I do not. _____

4. I mentally criticize the speaker's appearance,
    mannerisms, grammar, or speaking style
    while he or she is speaking. _____

5. I decide that what the speaker is saying
    is not of interest to me. _____

6. I fake giving the person attention. _____

7. I do something else while listening
    (e.g., look over the person's shoulder,
    listen to other conversations,
    think about something else). _____

8. I interrupt the speaker before he or she
    is finished. _____

9. I tune out the speaker if the subject is
    too involved or difficult. _____

10. I am distracted by highly emotional words. _____

If you answered "almost never" to at least eight of the questions, congratulations! But if three or more of your responses were numbers 1, 2, or 3, you might want to ask yourself what you've been missing—because you're not really hearing what others have to say.

During a workshop at Anderson's company, participants identified characteristics of good and bad listeners. Bad listeners, partcipants observed, never look at you, are self-centered and judgmental, think they're too important, and are unfriendly. In short, they said, "you can't trust bad listeners" and "you never want to do anything for them." On the other hand, good listeners are trustworthy and friendly. Not only do they look at you during a conversation, they convey the message that they think you are important.

A Word to the Wise

Let's face it, there are times when it's tough to stay focused on the discussion at hand. Maybe you're absorbed with your own concerns, or maybe you're overly tired because you were up most of the night with a sick child. As much as you might like to beg off and postpone the conversation, that's not usually an option when you're on the job.

So the next time you're in a professional setting where you find it almost impossible to concentrate, be smart: at least make the effort to appear engaged in the conversation. Why? Because to do otherwise is to appear disinterested in those around you. People who don't listen quickly develop reputations for not caring and being oblivious to the needs of others—and those attributes can kill a career.

"You will be forgiven almost every misstep but one. A listener must be all there," advises Nancy K. Austin, a California-based management consultant and columnist for *Working Woman*.

Polishing Your Listening Skills

You can improve your ability to listen—all it takes is concentration and commitment. Here are some tips suggested by communication experts:

Listen with all of your senses. Human beings have five senses: hearing, touch, smell, sight, and taste. Focus each of your senses completely and totally on the other person's words and underlying messages. During presentations, avoid such distractions as doodling (touch and sights) or chewing gum (smell, taste, and touch). In a selling situation, concentrate all your senses on your prospect and you'll "hear" more messages.

Take time to hear the total message. Poor listeners often make a habit of jumping in to finish a sentence if a speaker pauses too long. Another bad habit: becoming so anxious to share your point of view that instead of concentrating on the speaker, you're rehearsing your comeback. But if you hear only bits and pieces of what is being said, you run the risk of drawing the wrong conclusion.

Check out your understanding of what the other person means. Offer a parallel example of your own, or rephrase the speaker's message by saying something like, "Are you telling me that ...?" Similarly, if the discussion is an emotional one, acknowledge the speaker's feelings and show your understanding with a response such as, "You must have felt really upset."

Fight the urge to "set the record straight." Avoid responding to complaints and criticisms by telling people how they should feel or why they are wrong. Listen to what they are really saying. Before you begin to frame your own response, be sure you understand the main thought the speaker is trying to share and consider it from that person's point of view—not your own.

Give feedback that will keep the conversation moving. Phrases such as "good," "I see," and "go on," show someone you're listening and want them to continue the conversation. These phrases, called "prompts" or "cues," are short messages that indicate you hear what the person is saying, understand their message, and want them to keep talking. You also can spur the conversation with nonverbal signals, such as nodding to indicate agreement or raising your eyebrows when the speaker makes a significant point. (We'll cover nonverbal messages more fully in an upcoming section.)

Ask questions. Open-ended probes—questions that begin with words such as "why," "how," "explain," or "describe"—will elicit the other person's opinions, attitudes, and motivations, and reveal their most important needs to you. Closed questions, such as "Do you mean…" will elicit clarification. Other examples of follow-up questions: "What did you do?" or "What happened next?" Asking questions is a technique that not only provides you with valuable information, it enables you to control the direction and momentum of the discussion.

"At the end of the day, listening to people is not so much a matter of studied style as a mark of leadership," maintains Austin, the management consultant. "Leaders pay attention. Leaders are willing to authorize people to think, and they make that clear by listening. Listening says, 'You are smart and have important things to say; you are worth my time, go ahead; what a good idea.' "

Personal Polish Tip

If you're trying to establish a new professional relationship, encourage the person to tell you his or her "success story." Most people love to share their experience, and listening to their trials and tribulations can help build a bond that may make them comfortable enough to admit you to their "inner circle" of trusted advisors and colleagues.

COPING WITH CONFLICT AND CONFRONTATION

Effective listening can help prevent misunderstandings and may even stop arguments before they start, but to some degree, conflict and confrontation are a natural, and even necessary, part of life. There always will be people with whom you just don't click, people who resist you and your ideas. Often, they're the very ones who are most vital to your success—a valued coworker, your boss, or an important customer.

While few of us welcome confrontation, avoiding conflicts, overreacting to disagreements, or always "caving in" can sabotage your career, or at the very least, diminish your efforts to project a confident, powerful image. That's why it sometimes pays to face a problem head-on.

The next time you're confronted with a person who seems ready to pick a fight, or you're involved in a small debate that threatens to turn into a full-fledged argument, here's a step-by-step plan that may help you cope and keep emotions from escalating out of control:

- Don't interrupt. If you want the chance to express yourself, you must be willing to extend the courtesy first.
- Focus on the content of what the person is saying, not the emotions. That way, you won't get angry in return.
- Pause before responding. Answering too quickly signals that you haven't weighed the message and feelings.
- Make a statement of regret to show you are sorry that the person has been upset.
- Make an empathy statement. Say you understand; paraphrase the person's statement of the problem—and do it with sincerity.
- Let the person know which parts of his or her problem statement you can agree with.
- At this point, don't try to explain or defend whatever happened to cause the anger.
- Be calm, correct, and clear. Don't intimidate with force or threats, and don't cloud your points with unnecessary language—or the other person may be become defensive and stop listening.
- Focus on what you can do to resolve the problem, not what you can't do.

Recognizing When to Fight

"Sometimes you need to ask yourself, 'Is this worth fighting over?' " advise the editors of *Communication Briefings.* Here's their checklist of points to keep in mind:

- ✔ Don't engage a difficult person if the issue isn't that important. Also, if someone else can get the job done and deal effectively with the difficult person, get that person to handle it.
- ✔ Allow the difficult person to win when you want to build a relationship rather than prove a point.
- ✔ Don't allow the difficult person to win when you're in an emergency situation and you must act quickly and decisively. Also, remain competitive to preserve your organization's integrity or to defend a correct, but unpopular, decision.
- ✔ Get the difficult person to cooperate with you in a solution when your investment in the issue is high and you value the other person's viewpoint.
- ✔ Negotiate a solution agreeable to both parties when you have little time to make a decision and you have failed to compete or cooperate successfully.

Negotiating Know-How

When you hear the word "negotiation," does it conjure up images of cigar-chomping men, sleeves rolled up as they face a midnight deadline for settling a contract with workers about to go on strike? If so, you're not alone. Most of us are intimidated by the prospect of any kind of negotiation, because the very idea connotes an adversarial confrontation in which there are obvious winners and losers.

Like it or not, though, life is a series of negotiations. Whenever you, for example, ask your boss for a day off, or try to convince a colleague to meet or move a deadline, or persuade your spouse to pick up the kids after school, you're negotiating. Done effectively, with a measure of common sense and flexibility, negotiation can help both sides focus on what they want and find ways to achieve those results.

The best negotiators are good listeners "who ask questions and get the other side's map of reality," says Herb Cohen, author of *You Can Negotiate Anything*. The key to successful negotiating: diminish the emotional content of a situation. "You have to care—but not that much. Think of the situation as merely a walnut in the batter of life," advises Cohen.

The best negotiators take their time, he adds. "Teach yourself to say, 'I don't know.' In negotiation, as in life, style tends to count more than substance. It's not what you said; it's the way you said it." Some of Cohen's tips for reaching win-win solutions:

- Care, but not that much. "Gain altitude" on a situation and look at it objectively before you start making a deal. A mind free of emotional involvement is more relaxed and confident.
- Assume that your partner is unlike you. Concentrate on fitting your needs to your partner's motives.
- Don't argue. The best negotiation is mutual, voluntary coaxing. Your partner will be persuaded to do what he wants to do, in a way that works to your advantage.

- Ask dumb questions. You can't know everything, so make sure you know the extent of your ignorance. Listen, and look like you're listening. Let your partner tip his hand. Showing weakness can work to your advantage.
- Save the worst for last. Put off zero-sum propositions as long as possible. Maybe they'll go away.
- Make sure everybody wins. This is your goal and your partner's. Learn to work together to make it happen, and you'll cut more deals and make more money.

Because few negotiations are one-time affairs, the way you communicate in such encounters can make all the difference in your ability to maintain a necessary relationship. "Traditional haggling, in which each side argues a point and either makes concessions to reach a compromise or refuses to budge, is not the most efficient or amicable way to reach a wise agreement," says Roger Fisher, founder of The Harvard Negotiation Project. "There's always the prospect that each side would do better by working out an agreement."

Without communication, there is no negotiation. "But whatever you say, expect the other side to hear something different," cautions Fisher. His advice for communicating during negotiations: "Listen actively, paying close attention and occasionally interrupting to make sure you understand what is meant. Ask that ideas be repeated if there is any ambiguity or uncertainty. It's very important to understand perceptions, needs, and negotiating constraints.

"Understanding is not agreeing. You can understand the other side's position—and still disagree with it. But the better you understand the other side's position, the more persuasively you can refute it."

Giving Constructive Criticism

If you're a business owner or your job requires you to oversee the work of others, chances are you've faced situations where you had to tell someone they'd done something wrong. Most of us struggle with this kind of communication, often preferring to live with a mistake rather than confront the person and risk a "bad scene." To be sure, there's a knack to correcting someone without making them feel completely demoralized.

Sam Deep and Lyle Sussman, in their book *Smart Moves,* describe ten ways you can provide constructive criticism and correct employees or coworkers without discouraging them:

1. *Tell the person what event, behavior, or performance concerns you.* "In the staff meeting, when my boss asked for performance figures, you spoke up just as I was about to respond."
2. *Tell the person how it creates a problem.* "I could tell by the surprised look on my boss's face that she wondered why I, her immediate subordinate, would allow one of my subordinates to answer. Furthermore, I didn't want the data reported in the format you chose."
3. *Explain how you feel.* "I was embarrassed and disappointed that you and I don't have our act together well enough to prevent something like that from happening."
4. *Ask for an explanation of anything you may be misperceiving.* "Why did you speak up when you did?"

5. *Listen to the answer and suggest corrective action.* "Let's first agree that performance reporting is something I will do unless we plan otherwise. Let's also sit across the table from each other at meetings so we can pass nonverbal cues."

6. *If possible, involve the other person.* "Do you have any other ideas?"

7. *Secure a commitment to future action.* "Do you agree this is the best way to handle our communication at meetings?"

8. *Describe how you value the person.* "Fran, this was the first time I have felt anything but appreciation for your input at meetings. And I know you'll continue to be an asset."

9. *Let your words sink in.* Don't start talking about something else. It's often best to leave the person alone at this point.

10. *Follow up on the corrective action.* Reinforce your suggestions by finding an opportunity to praise the person's new behavior.

Personal Polish Tip

If you intend to put your criticism in writing, give yourself time to cool off before dropping your memo or complaint letter in the mail. Be sure your correspondence is addressed so that only the person your message is intended for receives it.

Responding to Criticism

When a boss or coworker criticizes you, is your first impulse to win the argument? If so, it's time to rethink your approach, say Thomas and Diane Mader, authors of *Understanding One Another.* Conversations that take the "I'm right, you're wrong," or the "I'm sensible, you're being unreasonable" position rarely lead to satisfactory solutions.

Here are the Maders' tips for responding to criticism:
- *Ask critics to explain their criticism.* Don't rush to defend your ideas or make a case for your position. Example: "What makes you think my approach was arbitrary?"
- *Let critics assert their ideas* and don't reject their opposing position. By making differences clear, you'll be a step closer to resolution.
- *Paraphrase their feedback,* which lets them know you respect their ideas and have taken them seriously.
- *Acknowledge that both of you may be right*—but you probably can't have it both ways. Then ask, "What can we do?" This will signal that you're ready to start working on an agreeable solution.

The Pros And Cons Of Apologizing

Mistakes happen and when they do, a gracious apology may be in order. But "I'm sorry" can work against you, especially if you routinely use the phrase in situations where there's really nothing to apologize for. Women especially are prone to peppering their conversations with meaningless "I'm sorrys."

Dr. Leslie Brody, a Boston University psychologist, says that's because "men and women react differently to failure." Research by Brody revealed that when men failed at a task, they attributed it to external causes—a lack of financial support or impossible odds, for example. But when women failed, they blamed personal inadequacies, such as lack of intelligence or hard work, as the source. Because they felt personally responsible for the failure, the women were inclined to apologize far more frequently than men.

Often their apologies are offered reflexively in the course of doing business: "I'm sorry to give this to you," or "I should have done more," or "I'm sorry, I didn't know." This habit of prefacing ordinary encounters with a cursory apology serves little purpose, except to weaken women's authority.

Breaking the "I'm sorry" habit can be hard, but it's worth it, says Joyce Dean, a San Diego-based business manager who habitually apologized for not knowing certain information, even though she was extremely conscientious about following industry trends. Finally, Dean recognized that she couldn't possibly know or predict everything. "Once I realized that an occasional mistake is part of the game, I stopped apologizing for mistakes that were beyond my control and to people who didn't warrant it."

While no one's suggesting that you avoid responsibility for a serious error, be conscious of how many "I'm sorrys" you say in a day. And if you're an overly apologetic gal, take a cue from the guys: don't accept the burden for failures that are completely beyond your control.

"Apology can be masochistic, self-attacking," says Dr. Barbara Levy, a Philadelphia-based psychoanalyst. "Many women have this pattern in our society. It's defensive. If you apologize first, what can the other person say? Underneath the apology there can be rage at the person you're apologizing to. You feel guilty. You're also protecting that person by taking the blame yourself."

Levy maintains: "There is a way of apologizing in which one doesn't become subservient; when one is strong enough, and can say, matter of factly, 'I made a mistake,' or other words that suit the circumstance."

Power Talking

How you say something can be just as important as what you have to say, so sharpen your vocabulary and tailor your tone to your message. For instance, if you want to be seen as a doer, respond to requests with "I will"—rather than "I'll try," which can make you seem tentative. Some experts even go so far as to recommend eliminating the words "I can't" from your vocabulary.

"Your words can make you effective, rather than helpless, obliging, not infuriating," suggests George R. Walther, author of *Power Talking*. The words you choose not only influence others, they can inspire in you the attitude necessary to get your goals accomplished. Some word choices Walther recommends: Instead of "I'm afraid I'll have to check on that," opt for "I'd like to check that and call you back." Don't say "It's just my opinion, I could be wrong," say "I believe we can do something here." And rather than "I guess I got lucky," say "I planned well and worked hard."

Just as the right choice of words will create a more powerful image, your tone of voice and timing send cues that can have a positive or negative impact on your audience. If, for example, you're giving a presentation designed to generate enthusiasm, your message will have more clout if you speak in a fast pace and punch out key words with crisp enunciation. Keep your voice upbeat, use lots of positive words, and express yourself with animated gestures.

THE RIGHT MOVES

Much has been written about nonverbal communication, commonly referred to as body language. The most important thing to keep in mind about this aspect of communication is that your nonverbal messages—your gestures and expression—must reinforce your words and intent. When they don't, you lose credibility and your cause may suffer.

"Even though people may not consciously intercept nonverbal signals, they react to them nonetheless," say psychologists Tony Alessandra and Phil Hunsaker in their book *Communicating At Work.* If your body language and your words are not saying the same thing, the authors contend, "it may condition others to look for double messages in their conversations with you."

Body language is another area of communication where women and men differ considerably. For instance, when women nod, they're not necessarily indicating agreement; they only mean "I hear you, you've got the floor, keep talking," observes Pat Heim, author of *Hardball for Women: Winning at the Game of Business.* On the other hand, when men nod, it's because they agree with what's being said.

Heim cautions women to be mindful of how posture, for example, can inadvertently undermine their intent by signaling insecurity or weakness. "Women tend to shrink when they feel vulnerable. They get small by pulling their arms in, hunching their shoulders, and putting their heads down," Heim observes. "Men learn all kinds of dominance displays as children, while women don't."

Everything from the way you stand or sit to your eye contact and facial expression—even your height—can affect how an interchange goes. Because body language sometimes works when all else fails, (one study found that only 7 percent of a message is conveyed through choice of words while 55 percent is conveyed by facial expression and 38 percent by tone of voice), it's worth your while to learn this language.

Here's a checklist of common body language and how it's typically interpreted:
- ✓ Someone who stands tall, back straight, is generally perceived self-confident, whereas a curved back and lowered gaze communicate a feeling of inferiority.
- ✓ When someone leans toward you during conversation, he or she is probably involved in the conversation and interested in you; leaning away conveys disinterest.
- ✓ A relaxed and open posture usually indicates a favorable attitude and status; legs uncrossed and feet placed together indicate a neutral posture. A defensive or closed posture usually involves standing with legs and arms crossed.
- ✓ When both arms are folded across the chest, the person in question is generally protecting himself or herself, or hiding from an unfavorable situation; in a face-to-face situation, folding the arms across the chest usually signals disagreement.
- ✓ A partial arm barrier, such as holding onto one arm at the elbow, may signal either a lack of self-

confidence or that the person is a stranger to the group. Women often disguise their barriers by gripping personal objects (a purse, for example), to create a feeling of protection.

✓ Someone who crosses their legs and arms while seated has most likely withdrawn from the conversation. This is also a signal used by women when they are displeased with their partner. "Locked" ankles generally signal a negative emotion or closed attitude.

✓ To project an authoritarian posture, women especially may try to make their bodies appear larger by putting their shoulders back, placing their hands on their hips, and facing a speaker directly.

✓ Placing the hands behind the back and standing slightly off-center from the speaker usually suggests a submissive attitude.

✓ Leaning the head and trunk to one side signals agreement; when a person keeps the trunk and legs straight but turns their head away from the speaker, or supports their head with their arm, it's usually a sign they're losing interest.

THOUGH THIS CHAPTER HAS ONLY SKIMMED THE SURFACE of a complex topic, our brief examination has revealed dozens of reasons for developing your own compelling interpersonal communication style. This "calling card" can help you

- project a more powerful, confident image;
- form good working relationships with everyone

you have contact with...even the most difficult
people;
- handle conflicts, crises, negotiations, and other
high-stakes situations with composure;
- understand the agendas others bring to a discussion so you can tailor your communications to
fulfill their needs and achieve mutually constructive results; and
- present yourself and your ideas with credibility
and persuade coworkers, bosses, customers,
employees, and other potentially influential people to give you their cooperation and support.

Good communication leads to better decisions, fewer
confrontations, and greater success in your endeavors. So
whether you're involved in building a business, making a
name for yourself as a community leader, climbing the corporate ladder, or dedicating yourself to volunteer ventures,
you'll undoubtedly experience better results and greater
rewards by mastering the skills covered here. In the next
chapter, we'll take these ideas one step further by discussing specific techniques for selling yourself and your
ideas to others.

Chapter 5

LET'S MAKE A DEAL:
The Art and Science of Selling

> *"Perseverance is a great element
> of success. If you only knock long
> enough and loud enough at the gate,
> you are sure to wake somebody up."*
> —Henry Wadsworth Longfellow

> *"One should have absolute self-
> confidence, even in the early stages
> of a career....Be willing to learn
> from others, but at the same time,
> appreciate the actual value of the
> knowledge you already possess."*
> —Sarah Bernhardt

EVERYONE SELLS—IT'S AN INESCAPABLE PART OF LIFE IN THE '90S. Yet too often we fail to appreciate the role that selling plays in our lives and how much this skill influences our success in almost anything we do. That's the purpose of this chapter: We're going to explore the selling process at its most basic level and in the broadest terms, in an effort to demonstrate why this ability can be one of your most valuable assets. You'll learn the secrets of sales leaders, plus we'll give you lots of practical advice and proven techniques for getting other people to buy into your vision and support your objectives.

Everything Is Sales

Much as some people resist any suggestion they're in the business of sales, we agree with a quip we once heard: "If you don't think you're in sales, check your pulse!" Because of societal conditioning, many of us don't recognize the sales process except in its most traditional form of currency changing hands. Expand that concept to include the exchange of ideas, plans, enthusiasm, and points of view, and pretty soon you realize that every one of us is in the process of selling something to almost every person we come in contact with. Consider this wide-ranging list of "sales" cited in *Success Workshop Folio:*

> We sell ourselves when we pick a potential life mate. We sell our neighborhood when we put our house on the market. We sell our town, our state, our region of the country, when we attempt to attract tourists or new business firms. We sell our local talents when we raise money for a new community theatre building.
>
> We are selling our own capabilities and experience when we present our résumés to a potential employer. And, in turn, we are selling our company when we interview a desirable recruit. Selling is not "sales" anymore.

While it may be true that the nature of selling is changing, many of us still resist the image of ourselves as salespeople. "For the longest time, I didn't think of myself as being in sales," says Robert Noltenmeier, vice president of Quadrant Communications Company, Inc., a graphic design and marketing communications company he helped found.

Though the traditional "hard sell" has no place in his business, Noltenmeier acknowledges that the presentations he makes to clients are, in fact, a pitch, however subtle. "In this kind of business, you are basically selling yourself, you're selling your personal chemistry with clients, you're selling your ideas, you're selling the fact you understand these people's business, and that you are a value-added service they truly need."

Just the same, Noltenmeier would never bill himself as a "salesman." Why? "The perception of sales people is very negative," he says. "And I think there are still many people today who wouldn't be caught dead near sales per se."

Noltenmeier's right. Historically our society has taken a narrow view of this profession. Salesman was another word for thief. As the *Success Workshop Folio* article observes, "The lingering movie image of the slick-talking stranger who comes into town and dazzles the bumpkins standing around the courthouse square—to say nothing of the farmer's daughter!—then sells them a magic elixir for more money than you could shake a stick at and skips out on the next train, lives on to haunt people in sales even today."

Selling Equals Success

Tarnished image aside, our world could not get along without selling, which has evolved considerably since the snake-oil merchants made their rounds in the Old West.

SELLING YOURSELF

Today selling is not as much about peddling a bill of goods as it is about building relationships—figuring out what people genuinely need and convincing them you're the best person to provide it. As master salesman Percy Whiting once wrote, "Selling, to be a great art, must involve a genuine interest in the other person's needs. Otherwise it is only a subtle, civilized way of pointing a gun and forcing one into temporary surrender."

Simply, selling is the act of personal persuasion—making others believe in what you believe in, and value what you value—and in that regard, it's an ability few of us can afford to be without. "Selling is the one skill that all careers have in common," says business consultant and best-selling author Carole Hyatt, who's currently working on a book titled *How Not To Be Fired* (MasterMedia, 1994). In an earlier book, *The Woman's Selling Game*, Hyatt presents the following scenarios illustrating why virtually every professional must develop a complete command of selling skills:

You will be selling when the product is you. At some points and in various guises, you are probably going to be looking for a means to advance your career through a job, a raise, or a promotion. What you'll be doing then is convincing people that they need you, that it will be to their advantage to use and reward you for helping them succeed. You'll be asking for what you want, and the way you will get it will be through your ability to sell yourself.

You will be selling a product. When your career involves tangible items—clothing, real estate, art, machinery, equipment, or supplies of any nature—your mission will be to move the items from one place to another at a monetary profit. You will have to do this by convincing people that your product is superior to others, and that buying your product will be beneficial.

You will be selling a service. When you have an intangible product to move, yours or someone else's service, you will need to know how to persuade people that the particular service will improve their lives in some way. You may be an adviser, consultant, teacher, or artisan, a service provider or an agent for somebody else. It's all the same. To get people to use the service, you will have to know how to sell it.

You will be selling a talent. If you are a writer, artist, actress, director, designer, or the like—someone whose need is to express an innate gift—that expression will be complete only when you have given life to your talent by moving it out of the atelier and into the marketplace. Persuading people to buy your talent requires the same skills as persuading people to buy your product, your service, or yourself: the techniques and strategies of selling.

SELLING LIKE A PRO

Whether you're pitching an idea to senior management, peddling a product, or marketing yourself, much of your success depends on the impression you create in the first few moments of that brainstorming meeting, sales call, or job interview. You never want to give someone a chance to form any conclusion about you other than the one you want, and the best way to control that is through preparation. Here's how one professional featured in *The Woman's Selling Game* explains it:

> Selling is always being what it is I represent…If I'm selling professionalism, and quality, I always have to be those things. I have to be a class act. I have to be organized and have quality material in my presentation. I can't afford anything slipshod in my appearance. I am very careful that my grooming is impeccable, and that my material is as perfectly organized as it is perfect in content. I pay as much attention to not having runs in my hose or spots on my dress as I do to showing work that is excellent, right down to the spelling and punctuation. I feel strongly that I have to be "on" every minute, because people buy an image as much as they buy a service or product.

In any selling situation, your goal is to create the foundation for an ongoing relationship. While that can be an incredibly challenging experience, the job of selling can be boiled down to a straightforward formula: *get and keep customers.*

How do you do that? "Concentrate on the basics," counsel top sales professionals. While that advice may not strike you as impressive, one of the ironies of selling is that when people fail at it, invariably they've overlooked the painfully obvious. Seasoned sales pros put a lot of stock in the basics and readily admit that when they experience a slump, one of the first steps they take to recoup is focus their energies on the fundamentals of selling.

Before going into any selling situation, you may find it helpful to review this list of what most pros consider the fundamentals.

Your Appearance

No matter what your ultimate aim is, every sale begins with you. "People first buy you and then your product, service, or company," observes Terry L. Booton, author of *Cracking New Accounts*.

Because poor personal appearance can undermine you in so many ways, appropriate attire, clean and freshly pressed, polished shoes, well-groomed hair and nails are an absolute must. Most professionals suggest you dress the part of the prospect you'll be meeting. If you're unsure about what to wear, forego anything flashy; it is usually best to err on the side of being too conservative.

Looking sharp is a positive reflection on you and everything you represent. Conversely, neglecting your appearance raises questions that go far beyond your fashion sense. It can cause people to wonder about the pride you take in your work and may even jeopardize your professional credibility.

Your Manners

Observing basic social amenities—a solid handshake, good eye contact, and a sincere smile—can go a long way toward building rapport and creating an atmosphere that's conducive to relationship building. Engaging in small talk before addressing the reason for your meeting also can help smooth the way. And remember to practice common courtesies like beginning a phone conversation with "Do you have a minute?"

But possibly the most important point of etiquette you should observe is promptness. Tardiness is almost guaranteed to get you off on the wrong foot because it says

"I don't respect your time." So if you absolutely can't avoid a delay, at least call before the appointed time to apologize.

"Punctuality alone will set you apart from the vast majority of salespeople," says Booton. And it will make your job easier, he suggests. Why? "Because all of your customers will be selling for you to their peers and friends, once they know they can depend on you."

Your Communication Style

The words you choose and the way you listen send a definite message about what kind of person you are to deal with—and that's often the critical turning point in sales. "In today's competitive marketplace, the sales person's responsiveness to a prospect often determines whether a sale is made or lost," says D. Forbes Ley, executive director of Sales Success Institute.

As many pros are quick to point out, because the differences in competing products are often negligible, buyers typically make their choices based on the value of the seller. You can increase your value considerably by developing a communications style that makes you appear confident, caring, and in control.

If selling is new to you, pay special attention to the finer points of nonverbal communication—because rookies are often undermined by their own body language. When you enter a prospect's office, walk with ease and purpose, and maintain a confident but relaxed posture during your meeting. Tapping feet, jangling jewelry, and the constant clicking of a ball-point pen are unconscious mannerisms that communicate your nervousness loud and clear.

Your Attitude

It's been said that the most important sale in life is to sell yourself on you. If you feel good about yourself and believe in what you're doing, others naturally will too. Simple as that sounds, sales pros swear by this homespun wisdom, insisting that a strong sense of conviction really will show up in your sales numbers.

Bottom line, a positive outlook and cheery perspective can work wonders, sales leaders say. It stands to reason that if you're not enjoying yourself, if you can't get excited about your product and the prospect of making a sale, you can hardly expect your customer to muster up much enthusiasm.

"Unless you're dealing with a life-or-death issue, don't be afraid to smile," advises Dorothy Leeds, president of Organizational Technologies Inc., a New York–based sales and management training firm. "A grim-faced salesperson isn't going to develop much rapport and consequently, isn't going to make a sale."

Jeffrey Gitomer, a North Carolina–based entrepreneur who gives seminars and lectures on sales-related topics, goes one step farther, suggesting that even humor has its place in a sales call. "It's the best sales tool I've found," he says. "Have fun at what you do, and make the prospect laugh."

Your Knowledge

One of the first rules of successful selling: is to be prepared. "Beside making you confident and putting you in control, thorough preparation lets your customers know you care," explains Leeds.

Preparation—researching and rehearsing your presentation—sets the stage for all that will follow. "If you know your product cold, you have the mental freedom to concentrate on selling. You may not always use this knowledge in your sales presentation, but it gives you the confidence to make the sale," says Gitomer.

Nothing beats preparation for building trust with a client because it's just human nature to be more comfortable dealing with someone who appears organized and speaks with authority. Doing the necessary homework, so you not only know your product inside and out, but how it compares with the competition, is one of the best ways to handle objections, which we'll cover in more detail shortly.

Your Reputation

The surest way to turn a sale into repeat business is to deliver on your promises, sales pros advise. This principle can be applied to virtually any selling situation—if you want a single encounter to blossom into a relationship, you must demonstrate your commitment to that goal.

Perhaps the most important thing you can bring to any new relationship is a good reputation, suggests Sherrill Y. Estes, author of *Sell Like a Pro*. "Prospects are influenced by what others say about you. Establish a policy of dealing with others with integrity. Keep your word with customers."

Failure to follow through on your promises is bound to hurt a relationship, and may even damage your reputation beyond repair—because if you let customers and clients down too often, word gets out about you. Equally important, if you make a mistake, face it. Don't try to blame others or concoct excuses. Although everyone makes mistakes, accepting responsibility when the fault is yours is one of the hallmarks of a true professional.

BEYOND THE BASICS: AVOIDING CLASSIC MISTAKES

Although the theory of sales can be summed up in a few words, putting those principles into practice can be tricky at times. Successful salespeople are the first to acknowledge that there are no magical formulas—because each selling situation is an experience unto itself—and that some of their best techniques have been discovered through trial and error.

So what does it take to become a top-notch seller?

Empathy and ego drive, according to David Mayer and Herbert M. Greenberg, who offered this definition of selling in the *Harvard Business Review* some thirty years ago: The successful salesperson must have a "balanced ego to need the sale intensely and yet allow [himself] to look closely at the customer and fully benefit from an empathic perception of the customer's reactions and needs." It also helps, to have persistence, resourcefulness, persuasiveness, motivation, personality, trustworthiness, patience, tenacity, intelligence, and honesty, say Marjorie Weiss and Jim Martay, publishers of *SELLING* magazine.

Once you understand what it takes to succeed, the next logical question for most professionals: Where are the pitfalls—what would make me fail? While there are any number of challenges that salespeople routinely face, ask a veteran seller to name the number one mistake in their profession, and more often than not, you'll hear these answers:

1. Talking too much—instead of asking questions and listening to the customer.
2. Forgetting the most important question— asking for the sale.

Let's look at these mistakes and some other common stumbling blocks that typically trip up newcomers to the selling process.

Questions, Questions, Questions

As we've observed, the nature of sales is changing. The marketplace has grown more competitive, and in the process, consumers have become much more savvy. Gone are the days of the bumpkins versus the fast-talking stranger—unscrupulous practices and empty promises don't cut it in these economic times, and any businessperson who doesn't recognize that usually doesn't last long. Nor are consumers receptive to the hard sell. Instead of hounding customers, most salespeople are taking a different tack, often referred to as "consultative selling." In this approach, the salesperson acts more like a business counselor whose goal is to be helpful, understanding, and supportive.

"You've got to focus on the customer's needs," explains A. J. Scribante, author of *Soar to Sales Success*. "Once you know what the customer needs, you structure or position your product to meet those needs." Sales consultant Gitomer offers similar advice: "Sell to help. Don't sell just to make money, but to benefit customers. They'll know the difference."

Consultative selling demands communication skills that weren't required of the traditional product peddler. "The prospect wants to know that you understand his problems and his business," says Jay Levinson, a small-business expert who came up with the highly acclaimed concept of guerrilla marketing.

How do you establish rapport with a client or customer? "Asking questions before you make your pitch is the best tool you've got," observes Levinson. "That way, you forge better relationships, which is key to closing sales." When meeting with a client for the first time, make a point of getting to know the person. Open-ended questions are your best bet—try to find out about his or her professional background and experience, likes and dislikes, goals and plans for accomplishing them. Your objective is to draw the other person out, to get a feel for how he or she thinks.

"A surefire way to start a conversation with a prospect is to ask, 'How'd you get into this business, anyway?' " suggests Levinson. "Everyone feels that his story is unique and interesting. Follow up with specific questions about problems and opportunities facing his business. Then, once you've outlined the general issues, ask, 'If you could get one thing from our firm, what would it be?' Nine times out of ten, the prospect will tell you exactly what he wants to buy. That makes the sales process a lot easier."

Booton agrees, and offers this advice, which we think is especially helpful to consultants and people who market to big business: "Don't beat around the bush and appear to be fishing indirectly for information if you are talking to the person who has the ability to make the buying decision. They usually see through the approach very quickly and wonder if you have a hidden agenda. Most people appreciate the direct approach because it gets to the issues very quickly and precisely without wasting a lot of their time. I find it is best to be very direct in questioning."

In his book, Booton presents numerous sales scenarios and provides examples of questions that will help you in different situations. Here are some questions he suggests for pinpointing a prospect's wants and needs:

- What are you looking for?
- If you could change anything (from the way it is now), what would it be?

- How can I help you?
- If I were to give you this for free, would you take it? (Then find out why.)
- What is your biggest problem, and what are you doing to fix it?
- Are you satisfied with your current vendor, product, or service? If not, why?
- Do you know what you want?

Listening Has Its Rewards

Open-ended questions like the ones Booton suggests have many benefits. But the most artful questioning in the world won't help you if you don't take the time to listen, to pay attention to what the customer is telling you. It's a simple concept that seems to elude a surprising number of salespeople. "Everyone has a story of a salesperson who refused to listen," observes Levinson. "My associate's wife went to buy a $300 area rug and the salesman started showing her a $2,000 broadloom—and lost the sale. If your prospect isn't doing half the talking, you're in trouble."

Learning to listen to customers is one of the hardest lessons a novice salesperson must master, but the rewards are well worth it. If you doubt it, consider this counsel from veteran sales leader Hyrum Smith, CEO of Franklin Quest Company:

My clients often ask, "There are ten other time-management seminars out there—why is yours the best?" So I prove it to them by inviting them to attend a Franklin Quest seminar. I can't remember anyone who wasn't sold. The secret: Listen to your client and find out immediately if you are wasting his or your time. We're often so anxious as salesmen, we don't even know if our product will satisfy someone's needs. Once you are convinced, the emerging confidence *triples* your energy to sell.

You may find it helpful to review the tips on listening we covered in the previous chapter, because in sales, as in many other situations that require savvy communication skills, a well-timed silence is just as important as talking. You can't possibly hope to position yourself, your product, or service to meet a customer's needs unless you listen. Knowing how to use this communications tool effectively can make all the difference in your sales success.

"You will be amazed at how easy the selling process is if you just keep it simple," says Booton. "Just ask the prospect the right questions and he will more often than not, give you exactly the information you are looking for. If you involve the prospects and let them talk, they will often sell themselves."

Conquering Objections And Rejections

One of the things that separates super salespeople from the pack is their tenacity, the willingness to make one more call in spite of the objections and rejections that confront them every day. You don't have to be in sales long to realize that not everyone you approach is going to buy. But coming to terms with the "nos" that are an inevitable aspect of sales is one of the biggest obstacles novices must conquer.

How do the pros handle objections? They welcome them! Because objections signal opportunities.

But if that's true, you're probably asking, why don't more people succeed in sales? Because overcoming objections can be a complex, time-consuming process that demands determination, patience, quick thinking, and diligent attention to detail. "It means more than just answering a customer's criticisms," says Gitomer, who goes on to explain you have to "listen to the prospect, think of solutions, and create an atmosphere of confidence and trust that results in a sale. *The sale begins when the customers says no."*

While "yes" is naturally what we all want to hear when making a pitch, short of that, an experienced salesperson would much rather hear a "no" than a "maybe." Why? "Because 'no' is a word you can work with," explains Hyatt. "You may think 'maybe' is a lifeline, that as long a somebody hasn't said 'no,' you have a chance. Not so.

"A 'maybe' leaves you in limbo, stranded, unable to move. You've no objections to answer, no points to parry. A 'maybe' is really to put you off or get rid of you. Unless you reshape it to a definite 'yes' or 'no,' it is a worthless answer you can't do a thing with."

Turning No Into Yes

Overcoming objections is largely a matter of practice. About the only time you don't have a chance at changing a customer's mind is when your production or service simply can't fill their need. Everything else is negotiable. "Overcoming resistance is like putting together a puzzle," says Booton. "You put the puzzle together one piece at a time, and you overcome resistance by resolving concerns one at a time."

Here are Booton's rules for handling objections:
  1. Create a relationship with the prospect. Listen attentively and show interest in what he says. Good eye contact is essential. Pay attention to

your facial expressions and voice inflection.

2. Anticipate and try to answer objections in advance. Develop and practice several replies for each type of objection that may occur.

3. Ask questions. You can never ask enough questions. It seems like it is always the question you don't ask that comes back to haunt you. Ask open-ended questions that make your prospect think!

4. Question to draw out objections. Listen to and fully understand each objection. Make sure you are on the same wavelength as your prospect. Clarify his response to ensure you fully understand what he is saying.

5. Verify that you fully understand the question or objection, then address it before you move forward.

6. Avoid the use of the word "I," which makes you the focus rather than the prospect. Keep personalities out of the conversation and the discussion focused on a business level.

7. Don't argue. That puts the prospect on the defensive. If you argue, you usually lose.

8. Avoid "Yes, but..." That puts you on the defensive.

9. Don't guess. If you don't know the answer to a question, admit that you don't know, but tell him you will get back to him as soon as possible with an answer. Write it down so that you do not forget to research the answer.

10. After effectively handling each objection, go for the close.

11. Keep calm, be observant, be alert, and remember that an objection is nothing more than an opportunity to close.

Want That Sale? Then Ask For It!

Earlier in this chapter we said that aspiring salespeople are often undermined because they fail to do the painfully obvious parts of their job. Nowhere in the sales process is that more apparent than when it comes time to seal the deal. Most people make this aspect of selling, typically referred to as "closing," more difficult than it needs to be.

"To be a good salesperson," explains Bob Popyk, author of *Creative Selling* newsletter, "you need basic skills, street-smarts, a little persistence, a fair amount of personality, and some common sense. You don't need fifty-five closes, a degree in psychology, or three different selling systems under your belt. *You do have to ask people to buy.*" (This same principle can be applied to other selling situations. You must ask for what you want—an appointment, contract, deadline, referral, agreement for a course of action, and so on.)

Popyk goes on to observe that "often, the real key to selling is *you ask, you get.* Sometimes the more you ask, the more you get. Some people are terrible presenters, horrible qualifiers, and the worst at customer rapport, but they're great askers."

What makes a great asker? Timing and delivery. "You must always be prepared to close a prospect if the opportunity presents itself," says Booton. "Closing an order is like a comedian telling a joke. Like timing the punch line for a laugh, if you move in too soon or too late, you could blow the whole thing."

That's why a lot of sales pros recommend a technique known as the "trial close." As the name implies, this technique is designed to help you test the waters, to see how near the prospect is to buying and to probe for potential objections so you can adjust your presentation accordingly to get the sale. Best of all, a trial close may be used at any time during the selling process.

"Unfortunately, trial closing is one of the most underutilized strategies in selling," Ley writes in *The Selling Advantage Newsletter,* "even though it is one of the most powerful. It can tell you when to ask for the decision."

The nature of the questions you ask distinguishes a trial close from the traditional close. "The trial close is an opinion-asking question: 'What is most important to you about our product or service?' " explains Ley, "while the close is a decision-asking question: 'Would you prefer the...or...?' "

Trial closers often experience greater success because they've made the effort to flush out the prospect's thoughts and feelings well in advance of actually asking for the sale. "Often a salesperson experiences new objections when he is trying to close the sale. This is usually because the prospect wasn't encouraged to express his feelings about the product or service during the discussion," observes Ley.

Proponents of the trial close tout it as a low-risk strategy that can be especially effective for novices because it eases fears about timing. "If you're not trial closing, you may try to close before the prospect is ready to buy. Once a negative response is given, people can feel compelled to defend it and you're now stuck with a premature objection," cautions Ley. "Closing too late, on the other hand, can be as big a problem. You have overstayed your welcome and perhaps missed your opportunity."

Advocates of trial closing recommend doing it often and early in the selling process, so you don't risk missing that moment when the prospect's excitement and desire are at a peak and most of the objections have been put to rest. With practice, you'll learn to recognize the right time to ask for the sale because the prospect will send you "buying signals"—verbal and nonverbal cues that communicate a change of attitude. For example, the prospect may lean forward, or her tone of voice will change, or her eyes will light up, or she'll even begin to share her own ideas for how to use your product or service.

"Don't be afraid of finding out what the prospect is thinking and feeling," advises Ley. "If you use trial closes throughout the interview, chances are you will have learned long before the close just what the prospect wants, thinks, and expects of you…and the close can become the logical end to the discussion."

It's a Numbers Game

Despite your best efforts, you're going to be turned away sometimes. Sales pros don't expect to make a deal with every customer they approach and they've trained themselves to accept—and even appreciate—rejection by putting it in perspective.

The first thing any seasoned seller will tell you about rejection: Never take it personally. "They're not rejecting you; they're just rejecting your offer," counsels Gitomer.

Lastly, sales pros understand the power of persistence. "It's a numbers game—the more 'nos' you hear, the closer you are to a 'yes'," says Diane M. Wildowsky, director of her own telemarketing firm, Cold Call Enterprises. When she's having a hard time keeping the faith, Wildowsky reminds herself that:

- 80 percent of all sales are made on the fifth call;
- only 10 percent of all salespeople keep on phoning to the fifth call; and
- 10 percent of all salespeople make 80 percent of all sales!

Make no mistake, persistence does pay off. That's why you need to "learn to take 'no' as a challenge instead of a rejection," suggests Gitomer. "Be willing to persist through as many meetings as it takes to make the sale."

SUPER TIPS:
STRATEGIES OF TOP ACHIEVERS

Once you have a firm grasp on the basics and you're aware of the situations that are likely to trip you up, the next step is to get out there and start making sales. Don't worry if you don't feel ready. Lots of veteran salespeople routinely psyche themselves up before going out to meet customers. So push whatever reluctance you feel aside, because selling is one profession you can't practice in solitude. Remember, without the customer, there is no sale.

Knowing the effort and energy it takes to sell, and appreciating how discouraging it can be when you stumble—and you will, because even the experts bungle a sale from time to time—we've put together a list of super tips: bits of wisdom and tried-and-true tactics that veteran salespeople swear give them their extra edge. We hope they'll do the same for you. So give this list a glance now, but more importantly, keep your super tips handy for those times when you're feeling particularly frustrated and you need a pep talk, or you hit a slump and you're fresh out of ideas. These suggestions are sure to give you a boost and get you back in the selling mood:

"You must be self-motivated if you are going to be really successful," says Booton. "Many times you have to create your own opportunity. Success in sales is no different than success in sports. First you have to visualize being successful in your mind. Then you have to visualize making the call. Once you have gone over it in your mind enough times, you then need to execute the call. It is only a matter of doing it! After a while, it will become second nature to you."

"Be creative," advises Gitomer. "Once you learn the fundamentals, use your creativity and imagination to set yourself apart from the competition. Sound simple? It is...it just isn't easy."

"Treat everyone you meet as if he or she is the most important person you'll meet that day," suggests Roger Dawson in his book *Secrets of Power Persuasion*. "Even if you find it difficult to do at first, people really will become important to you once you've acquired the habit."

"Every time you meet with a client, ask him if he knows anyone else who might benefit from your services," suggests Levinson. "When you call the prospect, mentioning your other customer should make it infinitely easier to get in the door."

"Sell benefits, not features," says Gitomer. "Customers want to know how it works; they want to know how it will help them."

"When you want to increase rapport with a prospect, mirror them," suggests Wildowsky. "If the person leans forward, you lean forward. If the prospect states a need, repeat that need. You'll be surprised at how much this communications technique will help you connect with the other person."

"Give a discount for prompt purchases," advises Levinson. "Many people have trouble saying yes to a large purchase. The fear of making a mistake is just too great to overcome. You can conquer that fear by creating a new fear—the fear of missing a discount."

"Create an ad for yourself—a tagline you can use in person, print, or on the phone," says Wildowsky. "Your goal is to be remembered and referred, so make your tagline interesting, but resist the urge to get gimmicky." Wildowsky's company and tagline: *Cold Call Enterprises—your direct line to decision makers. We help you grow your business.*

"Create a notebook filled with laminated letters of recommendations from your clients," says Levinson. "These testimonials, from real people, on real letterhead, are worth their weight in gold. Prospects know that you can't buy a glowing testimonial for any amount of money, and they're inclined to trust someone who has the ability to show them one positive letter after another."

"Tell your customers and prospects that you want their business," advises John R. Graham, president of his own marketing services and sales consulting firm. "Don't ever assume that they know. Don't think that price is all they care about. Show appreciation. A short thank-you note may be far more effective than a pair of tickets to a professional basketball game."

WHATEVER YOUR PROFESSIONAL OR PERSONAL AMBITIONS, YOU stand a better chance of getting what you want when you understand the selling process and know how to use it to your advantage. The ability to sell yourself can advance your endeavors and enhance your life in ways that might surprise you. No one knows that better than this book's co-author, Kathy Thebo. As a teenager, she was so painfully shy she could barely speak up in class; today she's an award-winning Avon sales representative whose accomplishments have earned her invitations to be interviewed on TV and make other public appearances.

"Before I began selling, I was very doubtful I could do it," says Kathy. "I certainly couldn't imagine myself approaching strangers and striking up a conversation. But once I got into it, I was surprised by how much I enjoyed it.

"My attitude changed completely because the experience was so different from what I had expected. Despite my worries about being uncomfortable dealing with people, I discovered that if I did my job well, they were friendly and receptive. I also expected to have to push harder than I did for sales, but with each encounter, my confidence and expertise grew—and those feelings made selling easier, even fun.

"I've gone from being so shy I was almost tongue-tied to someone who can't wait to meet new and different people. But I would never have realized I had that potential, if I hadn't made myself get out there and do it!"

Isn't it time you made a sale?

Chapter 6

BLOW YOUR OWN HORN:
Ten Techniques for Successful Self-Promotion

> *Blow your own horn*
> *lest it not be blown.*
> —Mark Twain

> *I have been successful because I was*
> *willing to give up being anonymous.*
> —Sophia Loren

IT'S NOT ENOUGH ANYMORE TO WORK HARD. IF YOU WANT to get ahead, you also must work at the right things. Equally important, your efforts must be noticed by the right people. In other words, you need to sell yourself through self-promotion if you want your career to climb or, in the case of an entrepreneur, your company to stay ahead of the competition.

Simply, self-promotion is about visibility and positioning. It involves taking credit for your ideas and accomplishments, and making sure others are aware of and appreciate your personal assets—your talents, intelligence, and potential to contribute. It means making yourself memorable to people who are in a position to influence your future. Done successfully, self-promotion can establish, or even change, your image.

Despite the obvious advantages of self-promotion, many people have a hard time tooting their own horns. "Most of us have been brought up with the old messages that 'good work speaks for itself' and 'cream rises to the top,' " says consultant Jayne Wheeler. "But the truth is, unless we let people know what we do and what we do well, they are not going to beat a path to our door."

The prospect of self-promotion—whether it's vying for a job, seeking new clients, or soliciting support for a worthy cause—is so intimidating many people will do anything to avoid this form of selling. The reason is fear, according to George Dudley and Shannon Goodson, behavioral scientists and authors of *The Psychology of Call Reluctance: How to Overcome the Fear of Self-Promotion.* Their research found that natural self-promoters—people for whom the skill comes easily—routinely do three things well:

1. Position themselves, using current contacts and networks while constantly looking for ways to develop new ones.
2. Make sure they are seen and remembered.
3. Constantly repeat this process, never allowing any opportunity for self-promotion to pass them by.

"People who fail to self-promote are just as knowledgeable, talented, and skilled as natural self-promoters. They're simply stopped by fear," say Dudley and Goodson. The authors discovered at least a dozen reasons why people avoid self-promotion. Among them:

- constantly focusing on the worst-case scenario;
- obsession with image and credibility;
- fear of intruding;
- feeling intimidated by others because of inferior social standing or education;
- fear of mixing business with friendship or family;
- fear of asking for referrals; and
- fear of using the telephone for business.

Although studies show that men and women are affected equally by fear of self-promotion, it's generally agreed that women have a harder time overcoming their anxiety. "It's only natural that men can promote themselves with greater ease than women," career experts Jeri Sedlar and Rick Miners say in their book *On Target: Enhance Your Life and Ensure Your Success* (MasterMedia 1993), "A woman's socialization tells her from day one not to be aggressive, not to push herself out into the world, to be kind, soft-spoken, and nurturing. Men, on the other hand, have been encouraged to do just the opposite: Do whatever you must to get what you want—push, shove, hit your fist on the table!"

Consultant Wheeler agrees: "I think it depends a lot on your upbringing. You're somehow being a 'pushy broad' if you go out and let people know you're there. We need to learn how to promote ourselves in a way we are comfortable with." She adds this advice especially for women entrepreneurs: "You don't have to change your personality or your principles to promote yourself. You can do it in an ethical fashion that not only promotes you, but gets the business community to see you as a woman who is successful, capable, and competent."

Though you may never completely conquer your fear of self-promotion—many veteran salespeople admit to butterflies before every big presentation—you can curb your anxiety with practice and positive thinking. Remember, enthusiasm sells.

TEN TECHNIQUES
FOR PROMOTING YOURSELF

If the idea of self-promotion fills you with dread, don't despair. You can build a high profile without resorting to hype or glitzy gimmicks. "A great way to promote yourself is by knowing your business—the rules, regulations, organizational structure, plans, objectives, philosophies, projects in progress, inside information, financials, who's who, and all the miscellaneous," advise Sedlar and Miners. "Read the company handbook, directories, transcripts of the CEO's and president's speeches, annual reports, and anything else you can get your hands on." Much the same advice would apply if you have ambitions, for example, to sit on the city council: School yourself on key issues and controversies, and make an effort to become acquainted with the movers and shakers in your community.

Keeping current with your profession, industry, or community—depending on your goals—is an ongoing process that will support other self-promotion efforts. Although we've categorized the following techniques for the purpose of discussion, as you will discover, they are most effective when used in combination.

TECHNIQUE #1
Join Groups That Specialize in Your Interests

Organizations are one of the easiest and most accessible avenues for meeting prospective employers or potential clients and establishing alliances with people who are in a position to help you further your efforts. The opportunities to increase your visibility through memberships are almost limitless. Most professional fields have at least one association or organization. Don't overlook civic, religious, and social groups as places to make strategic connections.

One common mistake to avoid: investing in "ghost memberships." It's not enough to write a check for dues and read the group's literature each month—you must be prepared to actively enrich the organization. That means attending meetings, joining committees, and in general, contributing your time, talents, and resources to the group. Better still, look for ways to develop your image and skills as a leader: sign up for a special project; chair a meeting; spearhead an event. Colleagues and peers are most likely to remember you and perceive you as a worthwhile connection if you have demonstrated your value to the organization.

TECHNIQUE #2
Speak Up

If you're comfortable with public speaking, it can be one of the most effective techniques for boosting your visibility, building your reputation, and possibly even garnering media coverage. You also may want to investigate two organizations devoted to public speaking: Toastmasters International and the National Speakers Association.

Once you start offering your services as a public speaker, especially if you're willing to speak gratis, you may be surprised to discover how many outlets there are for this type of self-promotion. Community groups, fraternal organizations, and local trade associations, such as the Rotarians, have an ongoing need for luncheon speakers and people to provide programs. Such forums offer the opportunity to not only strengthen your presentation skills, but to demonstrate your expertise in a given field or to educate people about your business—without directly promoting it. The key here is to target your audiences carefully so you make contact with people who are in a position to respond to your message. In other words, if you're a politician and your goal is to meet voters, there's little promotional value in loading up your public speaking schedule with appearances at schools, no matter how much you might enjoy talking with young people.

"I find giving speeches to be a great way to get known and build credibility," says Gary Hennerberg, a Dallas-based marketing consultant. Hennerberg, like many people who rely on speaking engagements to help build their business, is affiliated with a professional speakers' bureau. Many such bureaus exist. For example, the publisher of this book, MasterMedia Limited, operates one primarily for authors.

You may want to consider being represented by a speakers' bureau if you're uncomfortable with the prospect of approaching groups and selling yourself as a speaker. Another advantage of speakers' bureaus: they expose you to a broader audience than you may be able to reach on your own. Many have the capability to book engagements throughout the country because they've developed connections with meeting planners and other professionals who work in the nation's top convention centers, where there's a steady demand for speakers.

If you sign up with a speakers' bureau, expect to give them a portion of your fee; typically, they receive a third for booking your appearance. Many speakers' bureaus won't sign you up unless you have a proven track record. You'll be expected to provide credentials, such as a video tape of you making a speech, and references, such as letters from organizations that have used your services and praise your speaking skills.

If the thought of taking the stage alone is too unnerving, you have a couple of options. One, volunteer for a panel discussion; these are widely used at professional gatherings. Another option: offer to lead a group discussion, preferably about your specialty. Again, such opportunities exist in a variety of arenas, including your church or temple, social clubs, and fraternal organizations.

Discussions are an ideal forum for the novice speaker because you gain experience in addressing a group without the pressure of feeling the whole show rests on your shoulders. Best of all, minimizing the stress of stage fright doesn't mean you sacrifice the promotional benefits of getting your name before the public. Conference literature, for example, will often include information about each presenter or speaker, which is a good way to gain recognition in your field—even among people who didn't attend.

TECHNIQUE #3
Capitalize on Conferences

Even when you're not on the program, gatherings such as conferences and seminars offer great potential for exposure because you can meet a large number of people in a concentrated amount of time. But you must be prepared to go where the action is and make your presence felt. In meetings, position yourself where you will be easily heard and seen; the front left-hand corner is the most desirable spot, according to one expert.

"My voice is very soft and hard to hear, so I always sit up front at meetings," says Kathy. "It also helps because I don't have people's heads in front of me, which can be intimidating and discourage me from sharing my ideas."

Being smart about picking her seat once put Kathy in the perfect position to meet the new president of her company. During a seminar discussion about a skin care product, Kathy shared her sales results—and it turned out she'd sold more jars of this particular product than anyone else at the meeting. "Because of that, the president noticed me out of a group of over a thousand people," she recalls. "He sought me out to ask my ideas and impressions on new products and sales techniques. If I had been too shy to speak up, this contact wouldn't have been made."

During meeting breaks or at the end of the day, mingle with fellow attendees and make yourself accessible by engaging in conversation. Two more hints for increasing the number of worthwhile people you meet at seminars and conferences:

- Obtain the list of attendees in advance (event organizers will usually provide this, if you ask). Familiarize yourself with the roster, making note of people you particularly want to meet. That way, if you're lucky enough to sit next to one of them in a session or happen to be introduced, you're more likely to recognize a name and be ready to make the most of your encounter.
- Arrive early and stand by the sign-in table. When someone you would like to meet arrives, simply step up and introduce yourself.

TECHNIQUE #4
Teach What You've Learned

You don't have to be a professional teacher to take advantage of the promotional opportunities associated with leading classes, seminars, and workshops. "More and more adult education programs rely on experience-based, rather than credentialed, teaching," says Barbara Winter, an entrepreneur who's created a seminar called "Making a Living Without A Job." Her seminar, taught nationally for several years, also inspired a book by the same title.

"Your own life skills could be valuable to others," Winter writes. "Problems you've solved, improved methods of doing things, data you've collected can be the basis for teaching and speaking in our information-hungry world." Winter shares the story of Kathleen Baxter, who was "in her forties when her therapist challenged her to start dating, something she'd never done. Kathleen had so much fun and success with her new social life that she now teaches a popular course called 'Dare to Date,' urging others to follow her lead."

Workshops and seminars are especially effective for entrepreneurs. In his book *How to Market Your Business,* Ian B. Rosengarten illustrates the potential of this technique, using the example of a hardware store. "If you have a hardware store, you could hold a workshop series for people remodeling homes. In your series, you could present experts demonstrating how to re-tile, how to wallpaper a room, or how to install windows," he writes. "This might attract those already loyal customers who are considering remodeling their home, or are in the process of doing so, as well as potential new business."

Workshops have proven especially effective for Kathy, who finds that teaching is a natural extension of her Avon business. "I have done hundreds of makeovers for groups using our beauty computer—which has translated into more sales and new customers."

Teaching is initially one of the most labor-intensive forms of self-promotion. It takes considerable time and effort to develop a presentation, and you'll probably want to create support materials to hand out during class. But in the long run, you'll get a lot of mileage out of that work because you can keep using your materials and repeating your same presentation over and over, as long as your audience changes.

One word of caution: While education can be a powerful self-promotion strategy, a poorly delivered presentation can damage your reputation, especially if people have paid to attend your seminar or class. One way to gain experience, test your topic, and perfect your presentation skills is to give short, free sessions with people you already know. For example, you might create a "brown bag" seminar that you offer during the lunch hour at your office.

TECHNIQUE #5
Put Your Ideas in Print

Writing for publication is a method of self-promotion that works especially well for professionals and entrepreneurs with service-oriented businesses. If you have a flair for writing, expertise to share, and the time to commit to getting published, you may want to produce
- articles for magazines or professional journals;
- a column for your local newspaper; or
- letters to the editor.

You can even create your own newsletter, a marketing tool that has proven effective for many small businesses. Or publish your own book. For example, we read about one enterprising woman who wrote a "How to Kiss" booklet, which she successfully sold through teen magazines.

Likewise, Pat Wharton, Kathy's sister, who's also an Avon sales representative, started a newsletter that she delivered to customers along with a sales brochure. "She made her newsletter appealing to the neighbors by including helpful information, such as local baby-sitters' numbers, as well as recipes and birthday notices. It was really clever," says Kathy, "but it was also a marketing tool designed to accomplish several goals—she wanted people to look forward to receiving it along with their Avon sales brochure and to get to know her better, as well as their neighbors."

"It worked. I'm convinced her business wouldn't have grown at the rate it did without this tool," says Kathy.

Writing often leads to other opportunities for exposure. Consider the experience of Miki Banavige, one of many entrepreneurial success stories shared in Winter's book. Banavige, who had started a business called Cooking is MAGIC (which stands for Making Any Groceries Into Cuisine), began gaining visibility by writing a food column for her local newspaper and teaching community education classes. From there, she moved on to giving demonstrations in supermarkets, kitchen stores, and department stores, and has since self-published two cookbooks, which she's now promoting with signings in bookstores and presentations at cooking schools.

Being published is an excellent way to increase name recognition in your profession, develop a reputation as an expert, or even carve out a new career. But unless you're prepared to self-publish, you should not undertake this promotion technique lightly—especially if you're targeting national magazines and major newspapers. Keeping up with the publishing world is a challenge even for accomplished writers, who regularly research markets, study mastheads, and peruse a wide variety of periodicals to ensure they don't waste time and postage submitting their work blindly.

One of the best ways to break in is to direct your efforts toward "special interest" publications, which generally focus on a single topic. "If you are a recognized name among those involved in a hobby, sports activity, or in your profession, you have an edge," says Elane Feldman, author of *The Writer's Guide to Self-Promotion and Publicity.* "For instance, let us imagine you are a collector of artwork, photographs, and memorabilia of fire houses, fire uniforms, and equipment, and that you belong to the leading organizations for like-minded people. If you would like to write on the subject for one of the special interest publications in the field, you would most likely be given a fair hearing."

No matter how knowledgeable you may be about your chosen subject, if you're not a professionally trained writer, study up on the proper procedures for approaching editors and submitting your work to publications. For example, before sending a query or manuscript anywhere, you'd be wise to check a book called *Writer's Market.* Advice on writing and publishing is readily available from numerous sources, including professional journals such as *Writer's Digest.*

If you are a beginning writer, don't overlook the publishing opportunities in your own backyard. Offer to help produce the church bulletin or to write for the local gardening club's newsletter. Small publications, such as weekly newspapers and shoppers, that can't afford reporting staff often welcome contributions from fledgling writers. This is sometimes true even on the national level. We know of one amateur writer who was offered a chance to produce a monthly column for a small writing magazine, provided she accepted a subscription as payment for her work. She agreed, because the situation enabled her to demonstrate her talent, to build a reputation as a columnist, and most importantly, to acquire a collection of bylined clips, which have since helped her gain the attention of more prominent editors and publications.

TECHNIQUE #6
Volunteer Your Talents

Volunteering for new projects within your company or department is one of the best ways to increase your visibility, showcase your abilities, and establish new contacts. Obviously, this technique is most effective if you direct your energies toward high-profile assignments. Even if your responsibilities put you in a behind-the-scenes role on a major project, don't discount the potential for exposure— very often you'll find yourself interacting with corporate leaders who might not otherwise have an occasion to see you in action and appreciate your talents. One employee at a New York insurance company recalls how her work on a high-profile project earned her the attention of a vice president, who sought her out at the holiday party to tell her how impressed he was with her performance. Although they had worked for the same company for several years, he'd never said a word to her before.

Becoming involved in organizations and your community also can boost your visibility. Trace the career path of almost any corporate leader and chances are, you'll find a history of active participation in charitable, political, social, and cultural groups. Why? Because volunteer work can be a great way to acquire skills that make you more marketable and promotable. Consider the case of Susan Pepperdine, a former supervisor of customer information at Kansas City Power & Light, who turned her volunteer work as president of the local humane society into a higher-level PR post at a marketing firm. Organizing such projects as her "Save the Elephant" campaign, gave Pepperdine critical bottom-line experience. "I also learned all about publicity, promotions and how to write a marketing plan," says Pepperdine.

Kathy had her first taste of making presentations when, as a young mother, she joined her local school board. "I didn't realize at the time that I would have to give a report at the meeting," she recalls. "But that little bit of exposure really helped me, especially as I became active in Avon and began to run my own business."

TECHNIQUE #7
Support a Good Cause

An extension of the previous technique, this type of self-promotion is especially useful to entrepreneurs who want to establish their image, because in recent years, the public has become increasingly conscious of how businesses give back to their communities. Volunteering a service or donating a product offers a twofold benefit: You can introduce your business to new markets while supporting the cause of your choice.

Long before Suzan Schatz of Tulsa opened her catering business, she was capitalizing on the benefits of community involvement. As a pastry chef at a local country club, she volunteered, for instance, to produce a dessert buffet for a charity benefit. "It was a good way to start," she says, "because, to this day, those people are some of my best customers." Later, when she opened her own business, Soigné Sweets, Schatz not only approached bridal contractors with her wares, she donated desserts to the local ballet and opera companies—with rewarding results: "That's how I got hooked up with the

wealthier clientele," she says. But the benefits of such dona-
tions cut both ways. Schatz says her favorite causes "are better off if I give them a cake to auction for $150, as opposed
to giving cash, which wouldn't be as much."

Kathy regularly donates profits from her Avon sales to
local charities such as the YWCA, schools, and organizations that support children. Her efforts have earned her a
reputation in her community. For example, when she
decided to raise money for a children's cancer hospital, the
local newspaper did a profile of Kathy under the headline
"Charity booster: Avon lady rings the bell for a good cause."

While there's no question this kind of press has the
potential to boost Kathy's business, her motives are purely
personal. She became interested in helping children with
cancer, for instance, after learning that one of her husband's coworkers had a daughter who'd been diagnosed
with the disease. "Before I sold Avon I did volunteer work,"
Kathy says. "This is a way I can give back to the community
because I'm working full time now."

TECHNIQUE #8
Position Yourself as an Expert

In their book, Sedlar and Miners tell how one plateaued
executive catapulted her career by promoting herself as an
expert. As a senior vice president for a financial services
firm, she had advanced as far as she could in her current
company, short of being named president—which didn't
seem likely in the near future. So she opted for another
course of action.

"During her climb at her company, she had become an
authority on her industry, but had never promoted herself
as an expert outside of her corporation," according to
Sedlar and Miners. "She took the initiative and hired a pub-

lic relations consultant, and also took a media training course. She promoted herself to television and radio stations, and was invited to appear on financial news features. She was also regularly quoted in the press. Her increased profile paid off—an industry headhunter started tracking her progress and within six months she was offered the top spot at a competitive financial services company."

If you have limited time for publicity, consider this tip from Feldman, author of the promotion handbook for writers: "Many radio shows do what are called 'phoners,' in which guests are interviewed on the telephone. If you are booked to do a phoner, you don't have to leave your home to 'appear' on the show—terrific for writers who are on a deadline." Feldman's advice is equally applicable to executives whose schedules make it difficult to get away from the office and entrepreneurs who can't afford to leave their businesses unattended.

Becoming a media star isn't as difficult as you might imagine, if you're willing to start small. Rather than going after national coverage right away, contact local papers and radio stations and offer your services as an expert. "That puts you in a position to be picked up by media bookers and reporters around the country who are hungry for new faces and interesting ideas," advises Gail Evans, a booker for *CNN*. To illustrate her point, Evans cites the experience of Pearl Polto, a Philadelphia entrepreneur. As president of her own credit advisory firm, Polto approached a local radio station, asking for a minute of air time to talk about credit fraud. After her spot, the station was swamped with listener phone calls. Now Polto is a *CNN* regular. "Aggressiveness definitely pays off," says Evans.

TECHNIQUE #9
Polish Your Networking Skills

So much has been written about networking that some people may regard it as "yesterday's news," say authors Sedlar and Miners. But they maintain this method of self-promotion is a reality most of us can't afford to ignore: "In the 1980s networking was a pipeline, in the 1990s it's a lifeline. In the midst of a dismal economy and widespread company layoffs, networking is no longer an option, it's a must. We don't mean networking in terms of just exchanging as many business cards as possible, but being and keeping 'in the know.' Being in the know means creating and keeping communication channels open in your job and the larger industry. It also means forming ongoing alliances with people you've known over the years—friends, family, college peers, professors, former coworkers and bosses, and members of organizations you belong to or once belonged to."

Networking is a practiced art that, when done in the right spirit, can yield a multitude of benefits, from job leads to media contacts to new accounts to advice about employee problems. Ideally, your networking connections are there to aid and support you. But too often, businesspeople assume the only reason to network is to increase sales.

"By its nature, networking means that you often have a business reason for wanting to talk to someone, but there are ways to introduce people to your products or ideas without turning them off," says Leslie Smith, associate director of the National Association of Executive Females. "The first order in networking is the same as it is in sales: Find out who needs what…in networking you're supposed to give first. If your attitude is 'What's in it for me?' you're not only misinterpreting what networking is all about, you're also not going to sell anything."

Networking is an integral part of Kathy's business. "With my wide customer base, networking really is my forté," she says. "I've helped people find baby-sitters, rent or sell homes, and get jobs. I really enjoy hooking up people who can help each other."

Susan Ashe, director of the Women's Resources Exchange in Buffalo, New York, says: "Good, effective networking is good selling, and there's nothing wrong with that. It's how you do it that can be a problem. If people feel used, you've gone too far."

Some practical pointers if you're new to networking:

- Develop a concise, memorable self-introduction. A simple, one- or two-sentence explanation is enough to spark a person's interest.
- Don't monopolize the conversation. Focus on others and encourage them to talk about what they do. People are more likely to listen to you intently if you show interest in them first.
- If you're shy, seek out someone who's standing alone. Very often, you'll find that person is a first-time visitor who's feeling just as awkward as you. Don't worry about rejection—most people will respond cordially when someone new approaches.

Personal Polish Tip

Create a "contacts file" of business cards you collect during networking situations. On the back of each card, write identifying information, such as when and where you met the person. You also may want to include a physical description or other key points, such as mutual acquaintances or interests you have in common.

In their simplest form, networks are simply people talking to each other and sharing information. But if you want to experience the true rewards of networking, talking alone won't do. You need to follow up, and turn your networking connections into real relationships. One of the best ways to do this is to practice the professional courtesies we covered in chapter 3. For example, send a note saying how much you enjoyed getting to know someone and then call later for a lunch date. And after the lunch, of course, send a thank-you note.

Networking works best when you take the initiative to stay in touch with and support your peers. For example, when you hear about opportunities that might interest your contacts, be sure to let them know. Similarly, make it a habit to clip and pass along articles so colleagues will know you're tuned in to their needs and interests. Some people prefer to set aside a couple of hours each month to flip through the Rolodex and call people they haven't seen in a while—just to say hello.

The point is to keep your relationships active. That way, if you need to ask for help in the future, your request won't come from out of the blue or seem completely self-serving. Likewise, don't wait to be asked for help. If you hear from a business associate that a mutual acquaintance is looking for a job, or needs a new secretary, or is trying to find a place to have a daughter's wedding, take it upon yourself to contact that person directly and offer your aid or a solution to the problem. Showing contacts that you understand the give-and-take nature of networking can go a long way the next time you turn to a colleague for a favor.

TECHNIQUE #10
Announce Your Achievements

None of the nine techniques mentioned previously will amount to much unless you're willing to sound the trumpets when you experience a personal victory. You need to launch a personal publicity campaign to ensure that your day-to-day achievements get the right attention from the right people.

"It's not enough to do good job or make the pivotal decisions," says career strategist Adele Scheele, "you've got to let everyone know." She suggests documenting and disseminating such news through memos. "Otherwise, how is the president going to know that it was your bright idea to save money using a computer consultant rather than training a whole department in the minutiae of programming?" If you're reluctant to sing your own praises, write memos congratulating and thanking the people who've helped you achieve your goals—and be sure to copy their bosses. Sharing the credit in this way not only helps build support among the people you rely on, it gives you an opportunity to subtly publicize your work among important and influential people.

Here are some other ways to announce your achievements so you receive appropriate credit:

- When you talk with colleagues, casually mention an interesting project you're working on or a beneficial referral you received or a new account you captured from the competition. This will help reinforce your image as an accomplished professional.

- If you receive special honors—an award or promotion, for example—send a notice to the editor of your company's in-house newsletter or to publications produced by organizations you've joined. Many of them have columns designed to spotlight members' careers and accomplishments.

- Share your fan mail. Let contacts know about the letter you received from a grateful client or the certificate of appreciation from the chairman of a committee. These are important milestones in the growth of a career or business, and you shouldn't be shy about celebrating this good news with networking friends and people who've taken an interest in your professional development.

SELF-PROMOTION IS A VITAL SKILL FOR ANYONE WITH AMBITIONS of rising to the top of their profession, building a booming business, or making a name for themselves in the community. Though your first efforts may feel awkward, don't allow yourself to get discouraged—self-promotion really will pay off. We've seen it happen in our own careers.

"I built my business slowly," says Joyce, "starting out as an adjunct instructor at New York University's School of Continuing Education, where I taught a course called 'Presentation Skills for Business Managers.' Now, many years later, some of those students are clients and a steady source of referrals!

"I also spoke pro bono to a number of groups, including the Financial Women's Association, Women Executives in PR, and Women in Communications," she says. "Those early contacts proved invaluable in getting my consulting business off the ground. Today I belong to those organizations and I continue to be actively involved because it not only benefits my career, but I find it personally rewarding."

Chapter 7

THE PERFECT PITCH:
Creating Press Releases Like A Pro

> *If you done it, it ain't bragging.*
> —Will Rogers

> *Though it be honest, it is never good*
> *to bring bad news.*
> —William Shakespeare

ONCE YOU START PRACTICING THE SELF-PROMOTION TECHNIQUES we've described, you'll probably have an occasion to approach the media for publicity. Sometimes characterized as "free advertising," publicity is one of the most powerful forms of self-promotion. But unlike some of the other techniques we've discussed, publicity is a little more tricky, because it's not completely within your control—you must capture the media's attention. In this chapter, we'll show you how to pitch stories to the media, using the tool favored by professionals: the press release.

129

The ABCs Of Generating Publicity

Garnering coverage from the press isn't as difficult as it may sound at first. Many small businesses successfully handle their own publicity, often achieving impressive results because they know their product better than anyone, they care about it, and they're willing to work long and hard to make sure it gets the exposure it deserves.

"All you have to do is learn a few basics," says Ira Davidson, assistant director of the Small Business Center at Pace University. For one, it pays to target your efforts toward publications most likely to give you coverage. Among the success stories Davidson cites is a hat designer who frequently sent photos of children's hats to *Child Magazine.* Eventually the magazine used a hat on the cover, and the designer's sales soared. "Being an entrepreneur often makes you interesting for the press," he adds.

The right kind of coverage can make or break a business, because one headline has the power to start a chain reaction. That certainly proved true for entrepreneur and author Barbara Winter, who shares this story about trying to interest the local paper in covering one of her early businesses, "The Successful Woman."

"Although I'd never written a press release, I got out my new letterhead and wrote to the editor of the lifestyle section of the paper describing The Successful Woman and why I thought it would be of interest to the paper's readers. I sent the letter off to the newspaper and held my breath. The very next day, I received a call from Ann Beckman, a reporter. She said, 'I have your press release here and what you're doing sounds interesting. I'd like to talk to you in more depth about it. When can I come to your office?' "

At the time Winter didn't have an office, so she offered to meet the reporter. "I had never been interviewed before and had no idea what it would entail," Winter recalls. "I arrived at the newspaper office nervous but wearing my best dress and trying to appear cool and collected. Ann turned out to be a wonderful interviewer, and we chatted away like old school chums for almost two hours."

Expecting a "modest little piece, maybe a filler buried in the local news," Winter was surprised to find her story "filled the entire front page of the living section." Nor did she anticipate the response to her story: "My phone began ringing immediately, and my first seminar sold out. The newspaper publicity also generated a steady stream of speaking invitations. In the first six months of The Successful Woman I appeared on local radio and television shows, talked to adult Sunday-school groups, appeared at every woman's conference in the area, taught in the university extension program, and even showed up as a 'celebrity' at a local telethon.

Two keys to generating publicity are creativity and finding a unique angle that will appeal to editors. "Editors are busy people who receive a blizzard of mail every day," explains Winter. "Don't be afraid to sell your idea. If you work for an organization, you need not limit yourself to announcing the club's agenda. Perhaps one of your club members published a book, was featured in an art exhibit, or received a prestigious award. Or, you may be planning an event at an unusual place, such as an historical monument, that could be interesting to readers. If you work for a business, you might want to announce such things as a promotion, a reorganization, special awards, unusual employees, special efforts in energy savings, or child care."

PUTTING TOGETHER
A PRESS RELEASE

Preparing a press release that will get results takes time and effort. The key steps for preparing a basic release:

1. Decide on your message.
2. Draft the release.
3. Send your release to the right sources.

STEP #1
Decide On Your Message

The most effective releases have a "hook." To appreciate the value of a hook, put yourself in an editor's seat for a moment. If they work for a large daily newspaper, they get hundreds of press releases every day, and may have no more than an hour to go through the whole batch. As a result, most releases are skimmed and judged newsworthy, or not, in a matter of seconds.

So don't make editors guess why your release is worth singling out of the pile—hook them in the first sentence. What about your product, project, or particular expertise will be of interest to readers or viewers? Are you the first to do something? Do you have a one-of-a-kind product or service? Have you turned up new information or developed a system that will change people's lives?

One good way to test your hook is to try stating it in a single sentence. If you can't, you're either trying to cover too much in one release or your thinking is fuzzy. For example, says Kathy, "My hook is that I was a stay-at-home housewife—extremely shy—who has been able to build a

successful business and spend time with my family."
Identifying your hook may take practice, but you can't
afford to skip this critical step because focusing your
thoughts will make the next step, writing the release, so
much easier.

STEP #2
Draft the Release

The content and format of press releases is pretty much
standardized, with some minor variations. To give you an
idea of what a professional press release looks like, on the
following two pages you'll find a sample from the press kit
put together when Kathy won Avon's Women of Enterprise
award in 1992.

Whatever your topic, any professional quality press
release should include these elements:

Contact information. Always include the name and
telephone number(s) of at least one person who will
be readily available to answer questions. Failing to
include a reliable contact could cost you coverage: A
nationwide survey of 25,000-plus circulation daily
newspapers found that the most frequent complaint
about press releases is that the contacts are not available when editors call. You also may want to list an
address, especially if the release is about your business. The contact information goes at the top of the
page, in either the left- or right-hand corner.

A release date. "Immediate release" is commonly
used. But if the information cannot be printed before
a certain date, be sure to note that.

WOMEN OF
Enterprise
AWARDS
—— 1992 ——

Contact: Alix Mendes
Avon Products, Inc.
(212) 546-7653

Maryann Stoll
Avon Products, Inc.
(212) 546-7484

FOR IMMEDIATE RELEASE

PROFILE: KATHY THEBO

Avon Sales Representative, Peoria, Arizona

As a child—even as her family moved from city to city to accommodate her father's frequent business transfers—Kathy Thebo was an "A" student.

That is, until she encountered one teacher's intimidating grading system. To get an "A" in this class, the student had to deliver three oral reports; two oral reports were required for a "B," and one for a "C." Thebo received a "D"—her first ever—and she was devastated.

So debilitating was her shyness, she explains, that the very thought of addressing her classmates provoked an almost physical paralysis. "I was probably more capable of building a hydrogen bomb, than standing up and exposing my self like that," she recalls.

But there is sweet irony in this painful adolescent anecdote. Today, the polished and articulate woman enjoys financial and social success that has made her a role model among her peers. "Open doors and talk to people," she urges hesitant new colleagues. "You'll be opening up a new side of yourself, too."

As Arizona's most successful Avon sales representative—her sales last year topped $125,000—Thebo is in demand as a keynote speaker at rousing sales conferences and awards celebrations, events often filled with a thousand or more faces in an exuberant crowd. She accepts invitations to speak to civic groups with alacrity and enthusiasm. Last year, she made her national television debut, appearing as a guest on NBC's "Cover to Cover."

- more-

AVON PRODUCTS, INC., 9 WEST 57 STREET•NEW YORK, NY 1OO19•(212)546-6063

134

But the metamorphosis she describes, and her victory over numbing timidity, was neither fast nor facile. Even as a young adult, married and with children, she would often shadow her husband at social events to avoid conversations with strangers.

Thebo had worked as a social security claims analyst, supporting her husband while he finished college. But as her family grew—she now has four children, aged 9 to 21—she wanted flexible hours, and more time at home.

In 1982, when an Avon territory opened in her community, Thebo's first inclination was to decline: pondering making unsolicited sales calls, the gripping old fears returned. But she plunged in and, despite her reticence, her sales grew steadily.

It was, in part, a family crisis that propelled her business to new heights. Having raised ten children, Thebo's parents faced financial difficulties, and her mother had health problems as well. "I wanted my parents to enjoy the retirement they had earned," she explains. So she recruited her siblings to help construct a mountain-view home on land she and her husband had purchased years earlier.

The importance of her goal, she acknowledges, overrode her lingering diffidence. The home was financed solely by Thebo's Avon earnings. But sadly, a year after her parents moved in, her mother died, though her father remains there today. "To have made my mother's last months happy is reward enough for my efforts," Thebo says.

Having accomplished this poignant objective—and with no pressing financial requirements—Thebo now channels a portion of her profits into charity, donating funds and products to the Foundation for Blind Children, a local YWCA and a home for abused women and children. "Ultimately, it's helping other people with their trials that helps you overcome your own," says Thebo.

# # #

Sample press release

135

A headline. While some people will debate the need for headlines on releases, we favor them. A well-crafted, clever headline can help capture the attention of an editor. But don't get so carried away with being catchy that you lose your focus. A headline should accurately summarize your story.

The main text. It's generally a good idea to write your release in the "inverted pyramid," a journalistic style that organizes information in descending order of importance. Thus, all the vital facts—who, what, when, where—should appear in the opening paragraph, commonly known as the lead. The following paragraphs should provide additional explanation, such as how and why a product is unique. If you're not familiar with journalistic style, studying the newspaper will give you a feel for this type of writing.

Busy editors appreciate lively but clean writing that is free of unnecessary adjectives and quickly gets to the point. Forget fancy phrasing. Keep your sentences simple and your paragraphs short (no more than four or five lines). And always use the active voice. For example, say "The CEO announced," instead of "It was announced by the CEO."

As for format, here are generally accepted guidelines:
- Copy should be neatly typed and double spaced, with wide margins—at least an inch because many editors like to make notes in the margins. Be sure to indent each new paragraph.
- Standard 8½-by-11-inch white paper is preferred by journalists. You can also use your business stationery, provided the design of your letterhead is not elaborate.

- Limit your copy to two pages; one is even better, as long as you can cover your main points in three to five paragraphs.
- If you do a two-page release, end the first page with a complete paragraph. Then type the word "more" across the bottom of the page.
- End your release with either the digits "30," or three pound signs: "# # #."

STEP #3
Send Your Release to the Right Sources

Placement—deciding which media to approach—is at least as important as writing the release. Usually the more targeted your efforts, the better. While it is a common publicity practice to send general announcements to dozens or even hundreds of media, studies show the value of such blitzes is questionable, because most editors don't perceive the material as relevant to their readers or viewers. According to one survey, 75 percent of the editors responding said failure to localize the message is one of the main reasons why press releases miss. Localizing can produce dramatic results: a study of 174 localized releases found seventy-eight were published; by comparison, of 1,174 general releases, only eighty-seven were used.

Likewise, releases sent to positions, such as "Business Editor," rather than individuals, are likely to get a lukewarm reception. A survey of a hundred editors revealed that they felt the sender didn't care enough to make a phone call to get their names.

Doing some basic research and exercising good judgment at this stage will pay off in terms of time, postage, and results. Rather than randomly sending your release to all the media in town, make a few phone calls to ensure you're targeting your efforts toward the right sources. Once you've done this, you'll have a media list you can use for future releases. But you'll still want to call media contacts periodically to make sure your list is up to date.

Follow Up

After you send your release, it's a good idea to follow up in a few days with a quick call to determine if the release was accepted. These calls represent opportunities to strengthen your promotional skills. If a release was not used, try to find out why so you can focus future efforts where they'll be most effective. And of course, a thank-you note to the editor or reporter is in order if you do receive coverage.

IMPROVING YOUR CHANCES FOR PUBLICITY

When press releases fail to get results, the reasons are often embarrassingly simple. "There are three things you need to remember to give your story its best chance at getting in the newspaper," says Winter. "First, get your story to the right person. Second, meet the deadline for the appropriate section. Third, send complete information for story coverage and/or photo coverage."

Here's a quick checklist to help you avoid other common but easily correctable mistakes:

> ✔*Have you included instructions?* If your release is designed to encourage a response (you're promoting a seminar, for example)

then explain how people can enroll, where, and what the price will be.

✔ *Did you proofread your work?* Misspelled words or typos are a turn-off for most editors. Some even admit that making a poor first impression almost guarantees a release will be pitched in the trash.

✔ *Did you get your facts straight?* "Accuracy is the lifeblood of a newspaper," says one journalist quoted in David R. Yalc's *The Publicity Handbook*. "If a publicist gets the facts wrong, and we use those wrong facts, it's our responsibility. If a publicist makes enough mistakes like that, I'll consider him unreliable and I won't use his material."

✔ *Have you translated jargon and technical terms into everyday language?* Winning press releases are written with the audience in mind. That's why, as a general rule, it's best to avoid jargon. If you must use unusual terms, try to define them in a phrase or, at most, a single sentence. Otherwise, you'll quickly lose readers.

✔ *Is your information timely?* Editors say it's not uncommon to receive releases announcing an event after the event already has occurred. Also, if you're trying to get publicity for a product or service, you'll increase your chances of coverage if you connect your situation to the "big picture," because reporters tend to think in terms of trends and patterns.

Exploring Other Options

If you're uncomfortable with the prospect of creating a press release, you have two other options: a fact sheet and

WOMEN OF
Enterprise
AWARDS
—— 1992 ——

Contact: Alix Mendes
Avon Products, Inc.
(212) 546-7653

Maryann Stoll
Avon Products, Inc.
(212) 546-7484

<u>MEDIA ALERT</u>

AVON, SBA HONOR WOMEN BUSINESS OWNERS
FOR ACHIEVEMENT DESPITE ADVERSITY

What:
- Five courageous women—each an inspiring American success story—will receive the sixth annual **Women of Enterprise Awards.**

- A young entrepreneur will receive the first-ever **Women of Enterprise Teen Achiever Award.**

Who:
- Television journalist and best-selling author **Linda Ellerbee** will share poignant insights gained over 20 years on both sides of the camera.

Why:
- Since 1980, the number of women-owned businesses has grown by 96%. Women now own nearly 1/3 of all U.S. businesses.

Sponsors:
- Avon Products, Inc., a company that has provided earning opportunities for women for 106 years.

- U.S. Small Business Administration, which assists, counsels, and serves as an advocate for the small business community.

Where:
- The Waldorf-Astoria
301 Park Avenue at 50th Street

When:
- Friday, June 19

- Reception: 11:30 AM   Astor Salon
- Luncheon: 12:30 noon – 2:00 PM   Grand Ballroom

Interviews: Award winners are available for interviews on June 19 from 10:45 – 11:30 AM or by appointment.

# # #

AVON PRODUCTS, INC., 9 WEST 57 STREET• NEW YORK, NY • (212) 546-6063

Sample fact sheet

a personal letter. A fact sheet, as the name implies, is a straightforward listing of key points on a single sheet. To give you an idea of how one's put together, we've included an example on the facing page.

A letter also can be effective in pitching an idea to the media. In fact, some editors prefer them. "News releases in themselves don't catch my attention 99 percent of the time," says *Fortune* magazine editor David Kirkpatrick. "What do are highly focused pitch letters that show an understanding of Fortune's editorial mission, and how we are different from our competitors."

Although a letter doesn't demand the journalistic style of a press release, your goal should be the same: to pique an editor's attention immediately. Strive to make your points clearly and concisely. And limit yourself to information that's relevant to the editor's readers or viewers.

What we've provided here is a basic introduction to publicity. If you expect to be producing press releases on a wide variety of subjects, or you're planning to launch a major publicity campaign, you might want to consider consulting a professional.

GOING WITH A PRO

When your ideas exceed your expertise or the energies you have to invest in promotion, or your efforts aren't producing the kinds of publicity you'd like—either in quantity or quality—it's time to consult a professional. Hiring outside help can be as simple as finding a professional writer to produce press releases or as comprehensive as engaging a publicist or public relations agency to plan and execute every aspect of a promotional campaign. Either way, you'll want to hire your consultant carefully and, as with any business transaction, make sure you understand exactly what you're buying.

PR professionals offer two distinct advantages:

Contacts. Unlike the entrepreneur whose energies may be divided in many directions, publicity professionals make it their business to cultivate relationships with the press. The publicist's job is to get press coverage for a client. Their success depends on their ability to place stories in the media—and that's what makes them valuable to you.

Expertise. Unlike novices, whose publicity successes are often haphazard, public relations professionals are typically trained writers who become experts in planning and executing publicity campaigns. They understand the importance of timing and know how to structure a campaign so it supports a specific marketing strategy.

Here are several suggestions designed to help you avoid some common mistakes if you plan to seek professional help with your publicity campaign.

It pays to get a referral. Finding a good publicist is very much like hiring a doctor or lawyer. Depending on your needs, ask business colleagues or acquaintances if they've worked with a copywriter or public relations consultant they'd recommend. If that fails to turn up any leads, try contacting professional associations in your area and or go the library and look through directories that list writers, photographers, or graphic designers—whatever expertise you're seeking. *Never hire a "specialist" sight unseen.* Ideally, you'll be able to meet in person, but at the very least, insist on becoming acquainted with someone's work before you make any commitment. Most creative professionals have portfolios or "books," as they're sometimes called, that show samples of their work. When reviewing a portfolio, look for examples similar to the job you have. Also, ask the person to describe their work on previous assignments that had objectives similar to yours.

One hint: Stay focused on the expertise you need to hire. It's easy when you're browsing through a portfolio to get sidetracked by flashy graphics, for example. But these mean little if what you're looking for is a writer. Always request photocopies or actual samples that you can review at your leisure.

You can judge the quality of a professional by the questions he or she asks. For example, does the person want to see samples of your past publicity? One mark of an experienced professional is the desire to understand your business. The more questions, the better—because what you want is someone who's prepared not just to carry out your instructions but to suggest new ideas and better ways of doing things.

Before consulting a professional, spend some time identifying your goals. What do you want the publicity or promotion to accomplish? Is there a particular media or audience you want to reach? This kind of detailed analysis is essential if you plan to seek several bids, because in order to accurately compare prices and services, you'll need to provide the same set of specifications to every consultant you contact.

A clear focus also can save you time and money. Here's why: If you're confused or uncertain about what you want, it's very difficult for a consultant to effectively advise you. Meetings that drag on without resolution are unprofessional and often pricey because most consultants charge for time spent in meetings, whether or not your discussions result in decisions that move the project ahead. In the long run, you'll get the most for your money if you know what you want to accomplish and then look to the professional to supply the expertise necessary to meet those goals.

Know exactly what services you're buying before signing any agreements or handing over any money. Patricia Gallagher, author of *For All The Write Reasons,* cites the example of a book author who paid a publicity firm $750 in advance because the company said it would send her materials to the New York media. "She was disappointed to find that she only had two interviews on very small town radio shows...," says Gallagher.

Likewise, be skeptical of any publicist who guarantees specific results. "Frequently, a PR man will wink slyly and promise he can 'get you' *The Wall Street Journal* or the *Boston Globe,"* says Bob Bly, a professional writer, consultant, and co-author of *How To Promote Your Own Business.* "This is an unprofessional attitude and an exaggeration; editors are not tools of PR agents, and no PR pro can guarantee favorable coverage of your story in the press."

Author Feldman concurs: "Any publicist who tells you, 'It's not what you know but who'—or who nudges you with his elbow, winks and says, 'I can spread some money around and get you publicity,' is one you want to avoid....Publicity is free, and anyone who tells you otherwise is either not a professional, is ill-informed, or is a charlatan."

Feldman offers another caveat: "You might encounter a publicist who says you will only have to pay *if they succeed*, and further that they *guarantee* you X number of interviews per city. While this sounds enticing, be aware that they might indeed provide you with a quantity of placements but the quality may be severely lacking. Merely appearing on radio or TV, or in print is a waste of your time and energies if the show or publication is not right for you...or the audience is not likely to find your topic of real interest."

To ensure that you'll get what you pay for, reach an understanding up front of precisely what a consultant's fee will include. It's best to get this information, as well as deadlines and any special conditions of the project in writing. This is standard practice in the profession. Most agencies will insist on a contract, for their own protection as much as yours. If you're working with a self-employed individual, a simple letter spelling out the conditions of the assignment may suffice. The more complex the project, the more critical it is to put your agreement in writing.

Don't select a consultant solely on the basis of a low fee. You also should factor in talent, experience, and knowledge the professional demonstrates. For example, if you're hiring the services of a publicist—and not just a writer to produce press releases—you'll want to be sure the person has good presentation skills. After all, much of a publicist's work is selling you and your ideas, products, or services to clients. Because you'll be relying on your PR person to represent you—in every sense of the word—in all kinds of situations and transactions, make sure you find someone who fits your image of yourself and your company.

So how much should you expect to pay for public relations services? Rates will vary significantly, according to the expertise you're hiring and the part of the country you live in. Creative professionals, such as writers and graphic designers, charge in several ways: by the hour, by the day, or by the project. Most public relations agencies charge clients a retainer to cover services within a designated period; typically, retainers are charged monthly and, on average, range from $3,000 and up. As a result, many small businesses find it makes more sense to hire individual experts as needed and negotiate a flat fee for each project. Either way, it's not uncommon on large or long-term jobs, especially ones that involve design and printing costs, to be asked for a down payment, followed by incremental payments as each stage of the project is completed. (Again, it pays to ask around and find out what your peers have paid for equivalent projects.)

If you have a budget for your project, discuss this at the outset. This can be especially valuable if your funds are limited, because an experienced professional may be able to suggest ways to stretch your dollars or know precisely how your budget should be distributed to get maximum results for minimal investment.

Don't get carried away and overcommit. No matter how much you might like a consultant upon your first meeting, give yourself time to make a good hiring decision. You want to be sure you have the right professional for your project. If the person hasn't come to you through a referral, be sure to ask for references and check them.

Whether you're working with an individual or an agency, if this is your first project together, don't make promises beyond the immediate assignment. If you're pleased with their results, you can always continue the relationship—but you will have saved yourself from a potentially costly and uncomfortable situation if, for any reason, things don't work out as planned.

IF YOUR PHONE DOESN'T RING OFF THE HOOK THE FIRST TIME you send out a press release, don't get discouraged. Many, many people are vying for the media's attention, and as the experiences we've shared here illustrate, success in making headlines requires a combination of persistence and luck. Equally important, you must be realistic when setting your sights on publicity. You may dream of getting a call from Oprah Winfrey, but the fact is, an engaging feature story in your local paper, a profile in a professional journal, or even a blurb in a trade magazine could actually do you more good, especially if you're an entrepreneur.

When author and publicist Kate Kelly was invited to be in the book *For All The Write Reasons*, she was asked to show readers "something like the letter that got you on *Good Morning America* or *Donahue*." But, as Kelly later confided to readers, she'd never been on either show. "Despite that," she says, "my business is still very successful. Many of us are not promoting information that belongs on those programs (in my case, my information is too specialized to be of interest to a program that must serve a mass audience), but there are plenty of other ways to promote your business."

Kelly, who wrote and published a do-it-yourself guide for entrepreneurs called *The Publicity Manual,* started out by sending a simple two-page press release to the editor of a newsletter for restaurateurs. Her write-up was "nothing spectacular," Kelly says, "nor is the publication one that most people would have heard of, but it was for me, the perfect publicity: It was free editorial exposure to an audience that wanted to learn to do its own publicity."

Since then Kelly has received national exposure in publications such as *Family Circle, Working Woman,* and *Writer's Digest.* "It's been wonderful," she writes, "but the publicity I seek on a regular basis...is something simple in a trade publication newsletter or magazine where I can reach the buyer very efficiently and directly when he or she is most likely looking for my type of advice." To that end, her manual has been written up in publications for hair salon owners, alternative energy retailers, funeral directors, lawyers, management consultants, nonprofit association administrators, and many other professional specialties.

Though such publicity could hardly be viewed as glamorous, it's paid off for Kelly. "As you pursue publicity, you'll likely be surprised at the results," she advises. "A major interview you're looking forward to may bring few sales; other times, a small item can bring astounding results.

"One point that is indisputable though is that publicity breeds publicity. I sell many books because I am mentioned in the resource lists in many start-your-own-business books. I solicited few of those mentions; I was included because of publicity I had received elsewhere. The same will likely be true with your business. A story about you in your local shopper newspaper may well result in important exposure elsewhere."

Chapter 8

MEET THE PRESS:
Strategies for Mastering the Media

> *I am one person who can truthfully
> say, "I got my job through
> The New York Times."*
> —John F. Kennedy

> *In America, the President reigns for
> four years, and journalism governs
> for ever and ever.*
> —Oscar Wilde

WHETHER YOU'RE AN EXECUTIVE AT A MAJOR COMPANY or a volunteer in your community, chances are that at some point you'll find yourself face to face with a reporter. Dealing with the media is an important aspect of many professional positions, whether you're promoting products, championing causes, or defending a company's position. Yet the prospect of making headlines is an experience most people face with mixed emotions, largely because of the occasionally glamorous, but often stereotypical, portrayals of the high-pressure press.

149

Relax. Meeting the press can be enjoyable, even fun, if you're wise to the ways of the media. That's the purpose of this chapter—to help you see the world, and more specifically, your role as a source of information, from the media's point of view.

An invitation to appear on TV or to be profiled in a professional journal can be an exciting opportunity to enhance your image. But it also means work—for you as well as the person interviewing you. Your interviewer no doubt is facing a deadline and the responsibility of filling say, thirty minutes of radio air time with lively conversation or producing a two-page spread with photos for the local Sunday paper. Whatever the reporter's assignment, make it your job to understand exactly what he or she expects. The more responsive you are to the needs and interests of your reporter's readers, listeners, or viewers, the better position you're in to build rapport with the press and to avoid the kinds of blunders that result in a sense of betrayal, or at the very least, a disappointing experience.

"Appearing on television or seeing your name in print can be a thrill," says Sharon Johnson, editor of *Breakthrough Strategies,* a management newsletter for women. "But it also can be a nerve-wracking experience, especially if the topic is controversial."

"Planning ahead makes all the difference," says Johnson, who offers this step-by-step guide:

Establish the context. Ask the reporter where and when the story will appear. This tells you how much and what type of information you'll be expected to provide, and how much time you'll have for reflection. Find out how much time the reporter plans to spend with you, and whether you'll be the only person interviewed.

Write out your own questions. This technique helps you come up with interesting facts and anecdotes beforehand, and prevents embarrassing hemming and hawing during the interview. It also can spot trouble in advance.

Provide back-up materials. Don't be afraid to come to the interview with charts, reports, and other materials—as long as they've been cleared with your superiors first. No one expects you to remember sales figures from five years ago. It's better to be loaded down with paperwork than it is to put excessive trust in your memory and make a mistake.

Avoid jargon. Engineering terms, Wall Street slang, buzzwords in your industry might be self-explanatory to you, but not to the reporter and her readers. For the uninitiated, jargon is boring. (We would also add that acronyms can be confusing and meaningless unless you explain them on first reference.)

Watch the record. If you're not used to being interviewed, it's easy to get confused about what's considered "on the record." You may think you're just idly providing background—then be shocked to see everything you've said in print. As a general rule, assume everything you say will be quoted. Be especially aware of "throwaway" lines. Remarks that seem funny to you at the time may sound awful in print.

Be assertive. Reporters warm to people who speak up, especially if you bring up something that's important to the subject which the reporter has overlooked. If she doesn't ask you at the end of the interview, "Is there anything else that we might have overlooked or that you would like to stress?" say so. (We've found that it's best to volunteer this information, rather than waiting to be asked.)

Johnson's final piece of advice: "Make arrangements with the reporter to follow-up questions that may need more information, such as statistics you're unsure about. If something important occurs to you later, telephone the reporter and discuss it. Most will go out of their way to be accurate and fair." To that we'd add a word of caution: If you're dealing with sensitive or controversial material, it's a good idea to tape record your end of a phone interview so you'll have a copy of what you said.

In our experience, reporters are reasonable people, even though their ability to be polite and personable often seems in direct proportion to the proximity of their deadlines. You've no doubt witnessed this if you watch interview-style news programs and talk shows. Think about the number of times you've seen celebrities as well as more common folk cut off in mid-sentence by a TV interviewer watching the clock. While it would be easy to dismiss this abruptness as simply rude behavior, there's a lesson in that moment. Knowing what goes on behind the scenes and appreciating the reporter's perspective can help you package your information into an engaging story and become the kind of source who's in demand.

THE RULES OF THE GAME

Whether you're dealing with print or broadcast media, certain rules and practices apply. For one, the media is not "all-powerful," but they often have the upper hand. In other words, while you can try to solicit—or avoid—the interest of the media, the decision to tell your story is usually their's. Sources who have the greatest success with the media have learned how to play the game: They know what to expect, and maybe even more important, what not to expect when meeting the press.

We'd like to share some of the most valuable lessons we've learned in dealing with the media.

RULE #1
Deadlines Are Not Negotiable

Say you're an entrepreneur who's sent a press release about a new product to the local paper. A reporter calls to get more details. You suggest a face-to-face interview for the following day because you want to show the reporter your entire operation. But the reporter declines. He would prefer a phone interview because the story is due the following morning.

At this point, you need to be realistic: Deadlines aren't determined by reporters, but by the editors they answer to. As a rule, reporters have little power to negotiate the scheduling of stories and they're loathe to incur criticism for missing a deadline. So if you refuse to comply with the request for a phone interview, you risk losing the reporter's interest and possibly even the coverage. In some instances—when you are the only source for information or when the perspective you bring to an issue is so unique the reporter can't create the proposed article with anyone else—you may have some influence over the timing of a story.

But that doesn't happen very often. "When you work with journalists," says David R. Yale, author of *The Publicity Handbook,* "you move in a world of continual deadlines, where time is tyrannical." Yale offers this insight from one journalist: "Sometimes the press seems arrogant because we have to have information by an inflexible deadline. But that's reality."

Appreciating the pressure a reporter's under is just part of the game when you deal with the media. In our experience, the more willing you are to accommodate those pressures and abide by deadlines, the better your chances of building good relationships with press.

RULE #2
The Need for News Never Ends

Reporters and their editors are constantly on the lookout for stories. Many a headline can be traced to seemingly casual conversations at store checkout counters, chats with neighbors, and party repartee. Media savvy sources know how to use the media's insatiable appetite for news to their advantage.

If you find yourself in a conversation with a professional journalist who seems even mildly interested in your business, or a project you're involved in, or a civic cause you're supporting, don't be shy. This is your chance to gain image-boosting exposure. When trying to entice a reporter, your first step is to explain why a story meets the particular needs and interests of his audience. At this moment, your willingness to be an accessible source can greatly influence the reporter's decision to pursue a story—and may even determine the approach.

RULE #3
Every Story Has a Slant

Publications as well as radio and television programs typically have a stated purpose or philosophy that guides their choices of what stories to cover and how to cover them. Appreciating the conditions under which a story is being developed and responding accordingly will increase your value and effectiveness as a source.

This isn't as complex as it may sound. Sometimes it's simply a matter of being responsive on the spur of the moment, or sharing your expertise exactly when and how a reporter needs it. Say, for example, you're a florist and you receive a call from a reporter doing a story on Valentine's Day and the significance of roses. Chances are, this call will come when you and your staff are harried with holiday orders, so you may be inclined to put the reporter off. But if you're willing to take a few minutes to answer questions about prices and the pace of orders that day, you stand a good chance of seeing your business cited in the story. Better yet, if you offer additional, pertinent information—a clever anecdote about roses or some insight into the tradition of sending flowers—you increase your chances of being prominently featured in the article.

Seasoned sources understand the importance of assessing a story's angle. Newsletter editor Johnson offers this comparison: "A piece about the personal computer industry that's slated for the home section of a newspaper will have a different slant than one written for the business pages. For the first, you'll need to provide more examples of how families use computers in everyday life; a business article will require more statistics about industry sales and growth."

Failing to recognize a story's slant is one of the most common blunders by people inexperienced with the media.

Instead of working in partnership with the reporter to create a situation where both parties benefit, novice sources often get so focused on their ideas that they end up in a pointless power struggle. Determined to have a story told their way, these sources may refuse to answer questions or insist on returning to issues that clearly hold no interest for the reporter. These tactics result in a difficult encounter that diminishes the impact of the immediate story and may even discourage the reporter from future contact.

Rule #4
Not Every Reporter Wants to be Mike Wallace

If you've agreed to be interviewed, you have a responsibility to yourself and to the interviewer to make the encounter productive. So if there are subjects you cannot or do not want to discuss, make the interviewer aware of these up front. Be judicious in your use of "off the record." Contrary to popular belief, many reporters don't delight in cat-and-mouse tactics, and few stories lend themselves to the intrigue and investigative techniques routinely used by Mike Wallace on *60 Minutes.* "Off the record" is a response that should be reserved for questions whose answers clearly could jeopardize your career or threaten your personal relationships. While reporters generally will respect your wishes to declare a topic off limits, be aware that your ground rules could abort the interview if the information is central to the story.

Publicity expert Yale takes a strong stand on talking off the record. "No matter how well you know a journalist, even if you are friends, you should never expect to talk off the record," he says, adding this counsel from one corporate communications executive: "The press has a job to do.

Yes, there are many journalists who can be trusted to keep what you say off the record, but that's a crummy thing to do to them. You're asking them to not do their job."

RULE #5
It's Your Job to Get Your Point Across

Often, of far greater concern than being exposed is the fear that your key points won't come across properly because the reporter doesn't know the first thing about your area of expertise. It's not uncommon in the news business for reporters to receive assignments when they come to work, many times with instructions to produce copy that day. As a result, a reporter may arrive for your interview having done little more than scan your press release or chat briefly with the editor who's come up with the assignment. If that happens, don't despair and don't take it personally—this is simply the nature of the news business. Reporters are accustomed to receiving crash courses from sources and many of them are surprisingly quick studies if you'll give them a chance. Again, this is a situation where a partnership approach is far more beneficial than an adversarial or antagonistic stance.

RULE #6
Expect to be "Misquoted"

Some sources insist on seeing a story before it's published. In general, journalists are wary of such demands, and many publications have policies preventing this kind of review. However, sometimes reporters will strike a compromise by agreeing to let you know in advance the direct quotes they plan to use in a piece. This mini-preview offers peace of mind all the way around—the source doesn't have to worry about being portrayed inaccurately and the reporter reduces the risk that a source will decide, upon seeing the published piece, to make claims about unfair treatment or being misquoted.

"Feelings of being misquoted are usually unfounded," says Joyce. "Many quotes appear distorted when copy editors change the context of quotes within a story. But the reporter plays no role in this process. Also, keep in mind that all quotations are, by definition, taken out of context. Usually, it is a question of 'how out of context' they appear and whether you believe the new context makes the quote favorable or unfavorable."

Cooperation is the Key to Coverage

Despite common notions about the cutthroat tactics of reporters, in our experience, most of them are dedicated to doing a good job and work hard to develop positive relationships with their sources. If you play by the rules we've outlined here, your chances of developing good media relations are strong. Remember, cooperation can work wonders. Probably the two most important things you can do, particularly if you're trying to build a reputation as an expert in your field:

- Be readily available for interviews—or risk that the media will move on to the next expert; and
- Be receptive to the reporter's efforts—unless, of course, the proposed story misrepresents the facts.

"I always try to be as flexible as possible with reporters and photographers, even though I know the time I spend with them may not result in anything being published," says Kathy. "For example, I had an interview with a New York paper that didn't run, and a photo session with *Business Week* that never appeared in print."

Just the same, she advises, don't discount such encounters. "You gain valuable exposure to people who will remember how easy you were to work with," Kathy says. "Sometimes it's funny how things work out. I did an interview with a writer from *Parents* magazine and we got along very well, so when she was being interviewed on the NBC show *Cover to Cover,* she recommended me to the producer as someone who would be good to interview. Attitude is very important in these situations."

In another instance, Kathy's approach turned a potentially negative story into positive press for her business when a local reporter from Phoenix contacted her for an interview on direct selling. "Even though the article seemed to be saying that it wasn't all rosy being in direct sales and several companies really looked bad in the story, all my quotes were presented in the best possible light. I was even selected to have my photo taken with two of my four children. Our picture appeared on the front page of the business section—and it made my company seem to be the exception to the rule!"

Likewise, Joyce is regularly interviewed on such topics as how to design and effectively work with presentation visuals. Or a reporter may call asking for "three tips on public speaking." Queries like these cover only a fraction of what Joyce teaches clients, so she could easily become frustrated with not being allowed to discuss the full scope of her business. Instead, she welcomes the opportunity to see her name in print, however limited the coverage. "In the long run, repeated exposure is the best way to build my business, so I make a real effort to be the kind of source reporters know they can count on for a good quote," she says.

SPEAKING IN SOUND BITES AND OTHER INTERVIEW TIPS

Every interview offers the potential to enhance your image, depending on how you conduct yourself and respond to questions. Being interviewed may look easy, but it takes practice and preparation to come across naturally, effectively make your points, and maintain a measure of control over the exchange.

Here's how you can make the most of your next interview:
- Be clear about the message you want to share. You should be able to succinctly summarize it in two or three main points.
- Learn to speak in sound bites—short, easily quoted statements.
- Anticipate key questions that may come up and consider how you will respond. You may want to practice with a friend or with a tape recorder, since most people find that forming a response mentally is very different than actually answering a question out loud.
- Plan for the possibility of negative questions and prepare points that will turn them into positive responses.
- Mention your organization, project, or product by name, rather than saying "we" or "it."
- Use anecdotes to illustrate and dramatize your points. Stories will make your ideas memorable, as long as they're relevant, interesting, and develop a specific point.
- Tell the truth—always. Deception is an approach you can't win with.

Remember, you are under no obligation to speak with a reporter. So before deciding whether to grant an interview, balance the pluses and minuses. On the plus side: an interview can be an opportunity to reach an important audience with your key messages.

On the other hand, you can't control the reporter or the presentation of the story. Reporters aren't obligated to use your statements in a story, or even to file a story. The time spent in an interview may not equate with the amount of space a quote or story receives.

That's why it's best to focus on what you can control— your own input.

Techniques For Telephone Interviews

There are several advantages to telephone interviews. For one, they usually can be handled quickly. Another plus: you can have a "cheat sheet" of notes in front of you to ensure you don't leave out a key point. But the absence of face-to-face contact also has drawbacks. You cannot read the reporter's body language or get a sense of what notes are being taken, so there's a greater risk that the reporter will misinterpret or misunderstand what you say. Another challenge of telephone interviews is that the calls are often unexpected.

Here's a checklist Joyce created to coach clients on telephone interviews:
   ✔ Stay focused. Do not do anything else during the interview, however long or boring it may seem.
   ✔ Stand up during the interview; your voice will project more authority.
   ✔ Gesture during the interview. Highlight message

points with hand movements and facial expressions you would normally use to enhance your ideas.

✔ If your phone interview is being recorded or transmitted on the radio, assume that you are "on the air" from the moment you answer the phone to the time you hang up.

✔ If necessary, set a mutually convenient time to talk rather than taking the call immediately.

✔ Don't respond to questions too quickly. Think. Take some time before answering, then be deliberate.

✔ Do your homework.

Dos And Don'ts For TV Interviews

Television interviews demand a keen awareness of the medium. After all, TV is entertainment, so you must be prepared to present yourself and your ideas in a manner that will hold an audience's interest. Having offered that advice, let us assure you that making a good appearance on TV—even if you're an amateur—isn't difficult, as long as you understand the process and you've prepared properly.

No one knows this better than Kathy, who used to be so painfully shy that in high school she once took a "D" grade rather than stand up in front of her class and give a report. Today she doesn't hesitate to appear before television audiences that number in the millions, and she can even enjoy being in the spotlight, because she's mastered a few simple tips for keeping her nervousness under control. One of her favorite techniques when preparing for public appearances is to picture herself on stage or before the cameras feeling confident and self-assured as she responds to the interviewer's questions. "I'm a firm believer in the saying, 'If you can imagine it, you can do it!' " she says.

If you're invited to appear on TV, here are some dos and don'ts that Joyce created for clients of The Newman Group:

Do...

- Preview the program beforehand to learn how the host or hostess conducts an interview. Learn as much about a program as you can.
- Keep your voice at an even pace and your tone conversational. Visualizing yourself in a living room setting will help you act and talk naturally.
- Look directly at the person you're speaking to, whether it's the interviewer or a member of the studio audience.
- Call the host or hostess by first name at least once in response to a question.
- Assume that once the interview begins, your image is on the screen even when you're not talking. The camera could be focused on you for a reaction shot, so be sure to sit up straight, keep your expression alert, and rest your hands loosely in your lap.
- Use gestures for added emphasis. Gestures not only make your presentation more appealing, they can help burn off nervous energy. Keep gestures close to your body—above your waistline and below your neckline—and be careful not to cover your face.
- Know the length of the interview and pace yourself accordingly.
- Lean toward the interviewer to show your interest.

- Bring a prop. Whenever possible, use visual aids to enhance your presentation.
- Know your audience. Reading local newspapers will help you personalize your presentation for local audiences.
- Rehearse with a tape recorder and a mirror to pick up bad habits. Or practice with a friend.

Don't...

- Forget to get your key messages across, whether or not you've been asked about them. You won't get a second chance.
- Stare at the camera (unless instructed to do so), ceiling, or floor.
- Be afraid to say, "I don't know." If the interviewer continues to press for an answer, paraphrase what you've heard from other experts and point out that your expertise is in another area. Then explain what you do know.
- Lose your composure or fall into the trap of trying to defend yourself if the interviewer is antagonistic or hostile. Try to change the tenor of the interview with an anecdote: "Let me tell you about the first time I did..."
- Get trapped into stating your critic's position. Just answer, "I'll let my opponents speak for themselves, but our position is..."
- Use jargon and business expressions that are meaningless outside your management or professional circles.
- Speak in the third person. Avoid phrases such as "the company's position is..." Instead, say "Our policy is..." Personalize answers with your own experience whenever possible.

- Smile continuously. Keep your face relaxed and your expression natural. A smile is appropriate only when the conversation would normally warrant such a response.
- Repeat negative questions when being taped. Tape can be cut and you can be "quoted" out of context.
- Touch the microphone—it will cause static. Also, bending too close will distort your voice.
- Swivel or rock in your chair. Plant your feet firmly on the floor, either by crossing your ankles or by putting your legs together with one foot slightly in front of the other. Restless movements, such as swaying, are distracting to viewers and detract from your message.
- Be late. If you miss the deadline for a live show, you won't get a second chance.

We cannot overemphasize the importance of preparing for a TV interview, because the more you practice the more confident and capable you'll be at handling whatever happens when you're in front of the cameras. Consider Kathy's first TV experience: "I was supposed to have the last question during the segment. Well, the other person on the show with me took more than her share of air time and I could tell that time was running out—and I couldn't risk not getting another chance to appear on that show. Fortunately, things turned out all right because I had practiced my main points and I was prepared. So every time the interviewer asked me a question that could have easily been answered 'Yes, that's true,' I turned the question around, expounded on it, and managed to get all my main points across."

One final insight on television appearances: Studios are naturally fast-paced environments and you may find the hubbub unnerving. Don't be put off by all the activity and don't be afraid to be friendly. Chatting with the studio crew and interviewer while they're setting up the show may help you relax—and the rapport you build might even gain you valuable air time.

STYLE STRATEGIES FOR
THE TV LIGHTS

Because TV is a visual medium, the way you look is as important as what you have to say. "Words alone can't sell your ideas," says Kathleen Hessert, president of a communications company. "Television demands dynamic messages and style is as important as substance. You can succeed or fail on the first impression you create."

The prospect of facing the cameras put writer Colleen Sullivan in a panic after an article she and her sister wrote about trading lives earned them an invitation to appear on *CBS This Morning*. "I was exhilarated to have been asked—exhilarated, that is, for about three minutes, after which I was seized by my primary feeling: blind terror," Sullivan later wrote in a *Working Woman* article describing her TV debut.

"I wasn't so afraid of what I'd say or how I'd sound; I'm reasonably confident about my verbal ability. No, the terror was a pure and simple, visceral one. My face—with all its dark circles and chins—was going to be out there for anyone with a TV to see." Her solution: wear strong col ors and rely on the expertise of the studio's hair and makeup experts.

Similarly, authors about to embark on book tours often consult Joyce before appearing on TV. One, Wendy Leigh, author of *The Infidelity Report*, wrote an article about her session with Joyce for the British edition of *Cosmopolitan* magazine. "We met at Joyce's flat. I was dressed in my number one television outfit—a low-cut plum woolen dress—and wearing dangling purple earrings which looked like big ripe grapes," Leigh wrote.

"Joyce decreed that my dress was rather low, and that my earrings were far too distracting. She illustrated her point by videotaping me and showing me the dangling, distracting, low-cut results. I was convinced."

Joyce's advice to Leigh: "Remember, you are on the show to sell your book. So forget about being a star." That's a common temptation for people entering the limelight for the first time. But you should resist the urge to make a dramatic change in your looks. After all, you've been invited to appear because of *who you are* and what you have to say. This is not an opportunity to imitate someone else's style—you'll just end up looking awkward and the audience will notice.

Here are some practical pointers to help you look the part for your TV appearance.

For Women...

Makeup. Because TV's high-intensity lights tend to cause you to look washed out, makeup is a good idea. You don't need to do anything elaborate—everyday street makeup is adequate. If you normally don't wear makeup, at least dust your face with a light, translucent powder. This will help absorb perspiration and reduce the shine from the lights. A shiny face can be the sign of a nervous person. It will detract from your credibility and give the camera crew a difficult time when focusing.

If there is a makeup person available at the station, follow his or her advice. This person is an expert who knows what works best on that particular set. It's also a good idea to carry some light face powder with you, in case no one is on the set to help you. "I remember my first television appearance," says Kathy. "I was told they would do light hair and makeup, but I still brought my own makeup case. Well, I learned an important lesson: Be prepared to do your own, because the makeup people are extremely busy with the regulars of the show and they may not get to you before show time!"

Hair. Soft and simple styles are most flattering. For maximum eye contact, style your hair away from your face.

Jewelry. Avoid large and extremely bright pieces, which tend to flare when the light hits them and distort the picture. Also, large bracelets, rings, and watch bands can easily bang against the microphone or desk and create unwanted noise. Similarly, large, dangling earrings can be distracting. If you're not accustomed to wearing jewelry, don't try it for the first time on television. Remember, if you become a new person for your interview, it won't ring true with the audience.

Clothing. Don't wear white or light-color dresses, suits, or blouses. Also, avoid all-red or all-black outfits. Blues, tan, peach, and shades of gray work best. Small patterns and stripes have a tendency to appear too busy on the screen—solids are the most effective look on color television. If your clothing distorts the picture, the camera technicians will focus on other guests and you will have lost a valuable opportunity.

Personal Polish Tip

Never wear something new—because you don't know how it moves with your body and where it may pull. If you feel self-conscious, you'll look self-conscious and that jeopardizes your credibility. Look like the best version of yourself, rather than copying someone else's style. Dress for business, not a dinner party.

Shoes. White or light-color shoes make your feet look larger on screen. Darker colors are preferable. Likewise, dark-toned pantyhose look better than ivory or nude. Don't set a trap for yourself by wearing high heels if you don't usually wear them.

Hats. Joyce's preference is to avoid hats, but if you must wear one, opt for a plain color and avoid a wide brim, which can create a shadow. Your hat should not block any part of your face and must never be more compelling than your message.

For Men...

Suits. Avoid suits with stripes, checks, or small patterns. Medium tones in gray, blue, brown, or mixed colors work best. If you wear a black or dark blue suit, avoid light-color accessories.

Personal Polish Tip

Don't ever wear anything you wouldn't wear at the office—no matter what the interviewer is wearing. If you feel uncomfortable, you'll look uncomfortable, and the audience will not take you or your message seriously.

Shirts. Light blue or gray shirts work best. Off-white or pastels are also good. But avoid pure white shirts because they can cause technical problems with light balance.

Hair. Don't get a haircut right before your television appearance. Haircuts usually take a week to settle in. If you trust that your barber won't get carried away, you can opt for a light trim or razor cut.

Neckties. Vibrant colors, such as red, are preferable. Avoid checks or very small patterns. Bow ties have a tendency to move when you speak. A regular tie is your best option, unless you think you'll feel ill at ease. One caution: your tie is not the place to attach the microphone; put it on your lapel.

Socks. Wear the over-the-calf style so that when you cross your legs there will be an unbroken line of color. Nothing looks worse than bare legs—except perhaps white socks. Always match the color of your socks to your suits or pants.

Handkerchiefs. If you must have a pocket handkerchief, make sure it's fresh and unwrinkled. As for a breast pocket handkerchief, muted colors or off-white works best, and be sure to fold it neatly.

Jewelry. Large, flashy tie clasps, cuff links, bracelets, and chains should be avoided because they capture light, causing a flaring image that distorts the picture.

Makeup. Follow the advice of the makeup person. If one is not available to help you, just dust your face lightly with powder. This will help absorb perspiration and prevent a shiny complexion from the high-intensity lights. A shiny face indicates a nervous speaker and can diminish your credibility.

Pockets. Empty your pockets of loose change to avoid the temptation of nervously jangling coins.

Personal Polish Tip

Here's a tip for both men and women who wear eyeglasses: Opt for reflection-free lenses if you frequently speak before an audience. Also, avoid heavy, dark frames that could interfere with the audience's view of your face. Likewise, never wear dark glasses for any public appearance—they create the impression you're trying to hide something or that you have a problem with your eyes. You don't want your audience to become so focused on trying to figure out what's wrong that they fail to listen to what you're saying.

A Few Thoughts On Photos

If you're the subject of a feature story for a newspaper or magazine, it's likely the press will want to snap your picture. Often the photographer will arrive for the assignment with some idea of the shot the publication is looking for to illustrate the article. You could be asked to demonstrate an activity that typifies your responsibilities or to strike a power pose. Maybe the photographer has something especially creative in mind.

Feel free to act naturally, but don't forget to exercise good judgment if this is an opportunity to express your business or professional persona. For example, a creative professional, such as an art director, might be able to get away with a shot that shows her riding a tricycle around the office. But for most of us, a traditional pose is preferable.

Likewise, if you're going to be photographed in your workplace, take a quick look around to see if some tidying up is called for. Avoid unwittingly making endorsements with objects, such as soda cans, that may be on your desk or show up in the background of the photo.

As for your appearance, use the clothing and makeup tips for TV as your guide. Also, it's generally a good idea to avoid smoking during the photo session. And what about smiling: Will saying "cheese" cost you your corporate clout? Probably not, say the experts, because a smile is always more engaging from the viewer's perspective.

"When I'm asked to do a photo for a magazine or newspaper, I try to think of a fresh angle or something that will help make the article more timely," says Kathy. "For instance, I was approached by *Fortune* magazine for a photo to go with a business article. It just happened to be during the Desert Storm period, so I got the idea of having a photo taken with my National Guard customers. *Fortune* was so pleased with the results, they not only pictured me with the article, they ran another large photo in the table of contents. So I had two chances for the public to see my name and my business."

WE'D LIKE TO CLOSE THIS CHAPTER WITH A FINAL REMINDER about the importance of nurturing professional relationships, especially when you're meeting the press. Make a habit of sending a thank-you note after an interview— "even when it's only slightly deserved," advises Joyce. "If you want to keep the relationship ongoing, stay in touch by acknowledging any interesting or important stories by the reporter with a note or telephone call."

Chapter 9

CENTER STAGE:
Delivering Powerful Speeches and Presentations

> *There are two times in your life when you are totally alone: when you die, and just before you give a speech.*
> —Anonymous

> *No speech can be entirely bad if it's short enough.*
> —Irvin S. Cobb, journalist

THERE'S ONLY ONE THING WORSE THAN WALKING ALONE into a room full of strangers: being asked to "say a few words." Public speaking consistently rates as the top fear among Americans, according to most surveys. Yet the ability to make a good oral presentation is valuable in all kinds of situations and a critical tool if you have business ambitions. "Excellent communications skills are fundamental. The No. 1 skill lacking today is the ability to make a solid presentation," says Harvey McKay, author of such best-selling business books as *Swim With the Sharks*

Without Being Eaten Alive. "You can't make a sale if you can't make a presentation."

Executives aren't the only people who need to polish these skills. Most of us have many occasions to make presentations in the course of daily life—we just don't recognize them as such, so we don't take advantage of these chances to get noticed and get ahead. Can you relate to any of these scenarios?

- You must persuade your boss to hire another staff member.
- You must inspire a task force to reach a common goal.
- You've been invited to emcee an award ceremony.
- You must encourage someone to accept a difficult assignment.
- You must train employees in a new work process.
- You've been asked to represent your neighborhood at an important town meeting.
- You must persuade a customer to buy or increase an order.
- You must convince a committee to approve a budget or a project proposal.

Public speaking is an ideal opportunity to display your abilities, win support for your ideas, and make a strong impression on many people at one time. But if the thought of taking center stage gives you the jitters, take heart. Being a confident and dynamic speaker is not a talent so much as a skill that can be taught. Even the most shy person can master public speaking—all it takes is a little practice and the proper perspective.

176

People have long looked for ways to improve their oral presentations. Consider this from *The Peerless Reciter,* published in 1894: "Be perfectly natural. Get in touch with your hearers. Stand or sit among them, as it were, and talk with them; do not place a cold distance between yourself and them, and then speak at them...make gestures...where they are required. A few, well-placed and suited to the thought, are better than many given at random...express joy, sorrow, wonderment, fear, merriment, hope, despair, anger...according as these are conveyed in language."

That's still good advice today, and as many successful professional speakers will tell you, when you learn to speak effectively in public, your one-on-one encounters and conversations also seem to improve dramatically. In this chapter, we'll outline the steps involved in preparing a speech or presentation and teach you techniques for delivering your ideas with conviction. Plus, we'll give you plenty of practical tips, such as how to overcome stage fright, how to grab your audience's attention, how to take advantage of visual aids, and maybe most important, how to feel good about yourself so that you can enjoy the experience of speaking before an audience—whether it's one, one hundred, or one thousand.

KNOW YOUR AUDIENCE

The first step in creating a compelling presentation is research. Mark Twain once commented that it takes three weeks to prepare an off-the-cuff talk. Of all the research you'll want to do, none is more critical than finding out about your audience. We cannot overemphasize the value of this step. Misreading, ignoring, or worse yet, never learning the needs and expectations of your audience is a surefire way to sabotage your presentation. For example, it's pointless to prepare a dog-and-pony show with elaborate visuals for a client who's more comfortable with a roundtable discussion. Likewise, playing it casual when a prospect is accustomed to glitz probably won't win you an account.

Each time you prepare a speech or presentation, you should begin by addressing the major question that every audience, regardless of size, has: "What's in it for me?" Knowing the answer enables you to tailor-make your remarks so you reach the audience in a very personal way.

This kind of analysis isn't difficult, and with a little practice, it will become a routine part of your preparations. First, identify the main purpose of your presentation. Is it to

- inform?
- persuade?
- solve problems?
- arrive at decisions?
- sell a product or an idea?
- entertain?
- inspire?

Next, look at your audience with the intent of determining how that purpose can fit their needs. "All preparation can turn to disaster if the nature of the audience and the nature of the situation in which that audience gathers are not understood and taken into account," says Peter P. Jacobi, a journalism professor and writing consultant. "There's no better way for a speech to bomb."

Key points to consider when analyzing an audience:
- How many people will be attending?
- Who will be in the audience?
- What is their relationship to you? For example, are they colleagues or clients or competitors?— and what ideas, feelings, or experiences do you want to share with them?
- What are the demographics of the audience? For instance, is it a group of senior citizens, or collegians, or grade schoolers? And what is their work background, social background, and educational level?
- How were they selected to be participants? Is it a business gathering, an awards dinner, or the weekly meeting of the local Rotary?
- How much do they know about the proposed topic?
- What attitude might listeners have toward you, your subject, and your organization? Are they friendly or hostile to your position?
- Are you aware of any politics, points of view, local customs, or prejudices that need to be addressed—or avoided?

Depending on the situation, you may want to investigate your audience and the assignment even further. For example, if you're speaking at a business conference, it's a good idea to ask:

✔Is the audience's attendance voluntary?

✔What's the nature of the event? Will your speech be the primary order of business or is this an occasion for eating and drinking?

✔Will the audience be tired or fresh? In other words, find out where you fit on the program.

Is it a daylong event? If so, will you be speaking
first, or just before lunch, or just after lunch,
or last?

✔What is the event's planner looking to you to
provide—a diversion, a lesson, a sermon?

"A speech requires a sense of direction," says Jacobi. "It
must go somewhere. It is simply not enough for a speaker to
want to talk, to fill time with words. Too many speakers do
just that, which is why too many speeches are unbearable."

Personal Polish Tip

If you've agreed to speak to a group you're not familiar with, ask the person who invited you for the names
of a half dozen people who will be in the audience.
Contact them and determine their backgrounds and
expectations for the presentation. Then, be sure to
thank these folks during the opening remarks of your
speech. This is a gracious gesture that not only builds
instant rapport with the audience, it lets participants
know you cared enough to do your homework.

SHAPING YOUR SPEECH

"Good speeches say something," advises Joan Detz, veteran
speechwriter, instuctor, and author of *How to Write & Give
a Speech*. "And they say it in a way that's lively, interesting,
and memorable."

Crafting a powerful speech or a convincing presentation is largely a matter of experience, and you shouldn't expect to deliver a perfect performance the first time you take the stage. Consider the speaking career of Winston Churchill. Though this statesman's podium poise is legendary, as a young man he lisped and stuttered when he spoke. Once, during a key speech early in his career, Churchill even fainted and slumped to the floor! But he persevered, becoming one of the greatest orators of his time.

While Churchill's case is dramatic, the fact is, most seasoned speakers have committed a blunder or two at the podium. It comes with the territory. But you can avoid many of the common pitfalls, simply by planning carefully in the writing stage. The more prepared you are, the more confident you will be when you actually take the stage. At the same time, we're not suggesting that you orchestrate things to the point that you're too rigid to appreciate the spontaneous moments and interactions that often occur with an audience.

The most successful speakers are adept at "thinking on their feet," willing to take some risks, and blessed with a knack for reading the crowd and reaching out to their audience. In those respects, public speaking is a personal experience that can't be reduced to a simple formula. Still, there are many things you can do during the preparation of your speech to increase your chances of captivating the crowd with a dynamic presentation. Let's look at the key stages in developing a spectacular presentation.

Find Your Point Of View And Focus

In order to say anything of substance, you need a point of view. Then you must focus and refine your ideas until you decide upon a single theme or message. You should be able to boil your message down to one statement, less than a paragraph long, most experts advise.

"If you try to include everything you know," says Detz, "your audience will probably come away with nothing. So cut ruthlessly. Sharpen your focus, shape your message, simplify your material.

"Likewise, target your research and resist the temptation to cram your speech with statistics," cautions Detz. Audiences can't absorb too many numbers at one time, so pick two or three of the most powerful and put them in everyday terms that listeners can understand.

Organize Your Material For Impact

Your remarks should have a distinct beginning, middle, and end. Here's a simple three-step formula for outlining a speech:

1. Tell them what you're going to tell them.
   This constitutes your introduction.
2. Tell them. *This is the body of your speech.*
3. Tell them what you told them. *Your closing.*

There are many ways to structure a message. Lists are one of the easiest. For example: "Six strategies for..." or "Three benefits of...." You also can organize material chronologically or sequentially, if that's logical, given your topic. Use conversational phrases to lead the audience from one section to the next.

We've included some examples of linking phrases, listed in the general order you might use them as you develop your presentation.

- *which brings me to…*
- *With that in mind, I'd like to discuss…*
- *Our situation here at _____ is very similar to…*
- *Like Mr. Jones, I also felt that…*
- *I'd like to support _____ from three main aspects.*
- *I'd like to discuss _____ from three fundamental points of view.*
- *Let's cover _____ with three essential elements in mind.*
- *Initially let's inspect…*
- *To begin with we see…*
- *Moving to our next area of concern…*
- *Next we come to…*
- *To continue the sequence we have…*
- *Now let's examine…*
- *Our next important element is…*
- *Lastly, we have…*
- *Finally and most importantly we have…*
- *So much for…*
- *In a nutshell then…*
- *Looking back we see…*
- *On balance, we discussed…*
- *So let's now take an overview…*
- *Reviewing then, we've covered _____ and seen that…*
- *Having shown _____, I recommend that we immediately…*

- *The thought I'd like to leave with you...*
- *Overall, you must agree that...*
- *I suggest without hesitation that...*
- *Clearly our next step is...*
- *What I want you to take away from...*
- *It must be apparent to one and all that...*

Start With A Strong Opening

Your opening line should grab the audience. An example that comes to mind is the Avon sales manager who began a discussion on recruitment by saying, "I'm what you might call a professional street walker." Her remark, which might have been considered risqué in any other setting, drew a round of appreciative laughter from fellow sales professionals, and by acknowledging their common experience— beating the pavement looking for new prospects—she instantly established rapport with the audience.

A rhetorical question, an anecdote, a summary of the facts, or a quotation related to your theme are equally effective ways to begin.

"Don't worry if the grabber doesn't come to you at first—and don't let it stop you from beginning to flesh out your presentation," suggests Joyce. "Somewhere in the middle it usually comes to you. One of my favorite ways to create a grabber is to move the conclusion of a speech to the beginning and then paint a verbal and very visual solution to the problem. That way, as the audience listens to your presentation, every point they hear will just naturally click into place."

Use Repetition To Make Your Message Memorable

Studies show that within a half hour after a presentation, the average listener has already forgotten 40 percent of what was said. By the end of the week, 90 percent is usually forgotten. But repetition can improve retention, so the more you illustrate and repeat your message, the greater the chances your audience will remember key points.

Signal phrases also can help focus the audience's attention on the most important parts of your message. Saying, "What's important here," for example, or "This can't be overemphasized," or "If you take away only one thing from this presentation..." will alert listeners that you're about to cover vital material.

Watch Your Language

Keep in mind that you're communicating to the ear—and it's ten times more difficult to command the ear than to catch the eye. So forget flowery language and complex phrasing. Churchill, for instance, detested Latinate words like finalize, prioritize, and systematize.

Simple, declarative sentences are the best way to get your message across. Words like "you" and "we" will create a feeling of dialogue during your remarks. Likewise, speak in the active voice, using phrases such as "Let's do it," and words like "speed up," "end," and "plan."

Your speech also will be more listener-friendly if you avoid jargon, acronyms, and foreign terms. Whatever you do, resist off-color language, profanity, and any remarks that could be construed as prejudicial.

Use Humor Judiciously

You might try Billy Graham's approach: "I give them something to laugh at. Then, while their mouths are open, I give them something to chew on."

While humor can certainly enliven a speech, most experts recommend a light touch. "Go for smiles, not guffaws," says Detz. Witty one-liners, lighthearted quotations, and real-life anecdotes are much easier to pull off—unless you have true talent for delivering a punch line.

"I'm personally a terrible joke teller," says Joyce. "If I hear a joke and want to share it with my husband later, I have to write down the punch line—or I can't remember it. So I would never dream of trying to tell a joke while standing up in front of a large group. I much prefer to share a story."

Humor can be tricky for a number of reasons. If you're speaking to a cross-cultural audience, for example, you must be mindful that many kinds of humor get "lost in the translation" and that it's awfully easy to offend or inadvertently alienate someone. "So if you're going to use humor, make sure it doesn't disparage anybody in the audience—women, minorities, or whatever," counsels Joyce.

It's a good idea to try out humorous remarks you plan to use with people representative of your audience, because you can use their reaction as a barometer to determine whether or not to include a joke. "It's not easy, especially if you're inexperienced as a speaker, to master comedic timing—how long to let the laughter go on, how to recover if people don't think your joke is funny," explains Joyce. "So use humor with caution."

Dare To Give Your Speech Some Style

"More speeches fail as a result of being boring, than for any other reason," says veteran speechwriter Andrew Wilson. "And that is often due to an excess of timidity on the part of the speaker or the writer."

Don't be afraid to dazzle your audience. "Make some portion of what you say shocking, even it if means exaggerating your own beliefs or playing devil's advocate to the conventional view," says Edith Weiner, a futurist whose work involves many speaking engagements. "It is important not to waste people's time by telling them things they already know—even if you tell it to them in an interesting way. You want them to come away with a new thought or something that jars."

Personal anecdotes are one of the most powerful ways to reveal a point and convey conviction for your topic. When Brent Filson, author of *Defining Moment,* a manual on leadership, talks on opportunity, he often describes his deathbed reconciliation with his estranged father. As the story goes, Filson was complaining about the lack of opportunities in his life when his father said, "Son, you have opportunities. They're in your hand. Just close your fingers." Clenching his own cancer-withered fingers, the father continued, "Even now, I have opportunities—the chance to love you."

Make Your Speech Visual

There are a variety of visual aids you can use to enhance a presentation, including handouts, charts, overhead transparencies, videotapes, and slides. "Visuals should help your audience understand and retain the information you are presenting," says Joyce, "but they should never get in the way of delivering the message."

Detz concurs: "More speeches are ruined by audiovisual aids than are improved by them. Before using slides or other visuals, ask: Would this enhance the message or detract from it?"

Personal Polish Tip

If you'll be providing handouts of important points, be sure to state that in your opening remarks. Even if you plan to distribute such materials after you've finished (a method many speakers prefer because they don't want the audience reading or ruffling papers during their talk), letting the audience know your plans in advance will spare you later criticism for causing participants to waste time taking unnecessary notes.

The use of slides, one of the most common visual aids, is widely debated among professional speechwriters. In his book *You've Got to be Seen to be Heard*, communications consultant Bert Decker argues that a speaker's goals are met 34 percent more often when visuals are used than when they're not.

But many experts remain skeptical. One drawback of slides: they break the connection between the audience and the speaker, who typically turns away to read from the slide. "You have to train yourself to point to the visuals, but speak to the audience," says Joyce. Also, keep in mind that slide projectors and other kinds of audiovisual equipment frequently are noisy, so you want to make sure your voice projects above any background sound.

That's why sometimes it's preferable to paint word pictures to help an audience visualize and retain your message. A well-done story, for example, can drive home a point and is far more likely to stay in people's minds. If you decide to use slides, here are some dos and don'ts from Joyce:

Do...

- Translate data into a visual image, such as a pie chart or bar graph.
- Keep visuals simple enough for everyone to understand and large enough for everyone to see.
- Be consistent with your format. Your best bet: stay with horizontal designs and set copy flush left, with a ragged right margin.
- Use color to create contrast between your copy and the background. Darker shades work best for backgrounds. For lettering, stick to basic colors, such as white, yellow, orange, green, and blue.
- Use a blank slide to indicate a change of topic.
- Dim the room without turning off the lights completely.
- Place the lectern to the right of the screen.

Don't...

- Crowd the screen with information. Limit yourself to seven lines or less per slide, including the title. (Some experts suggest you shouldn't put more words on a slide than would comfortably fit on a T-shirt.)
- Use all capital letters. A combination of upper and lower case lettering is much easier to read.
- Overuse bullets, dashes, and stars.

Leave Them Thinking

People tend to remember best what is said last, so plan the conclusion of your speech as carefully as you plot your opening line. Effective endings reinforce your message and give the audience something to take away.

"If your goal is to persuade people to accept an idea and take action, your ending should include exactly what you want your audience to do as a result of your presentation," writes speech communications professor Stephen D. Boyd in an article for the *Public Relations Journal*. "If you're promoting a blood drive, for example, you might add after your summary statement, 'Before you go home from work today, make an appointment with our wellness department to give blood.' " Another example: "If your focus is to inspire people to want to perform better or work harder, a concise ending would be, 'Make a commitment to yourself before you leave this room to make one change in your life that will make you more effective in your occupation.'"

Whatever the purpose of your presentation, your impact will be longer-lasting if you conclude by tying all the loose ends together and exit on a strong note. Avoid closings such as "Thank you for listening," or even worse, "That's all for now," Boyd advises.

"The German mathematician Peter Dirichlet had a great understanding of how to tie everything together in a conclusion," writes Boyd. "After the birth of his first child, he wired a telegram to his father-in-law which said simply, '1 + 1 = 3.' "

PRACTICE, PRACTICE, PRACTICE

Once you've compiled your presentation, the next step in your preparations is to obviously rehearse your remarks. It stands to reason that you shouldn't accept an invitation to speak or give a presentation if you don't have time to practice. But don't overdo it. Too often novice speakers misunderstand the purpose of practice: It's not to make you perfect, but to make you familiar enough with the material that you're comfortable when you take the stage. Unlike an actor or a singer, who must rehearse and rehearse until they have every word down pat and every move precisely timed in order to deliver a believable performance, you actually run the risk of losing credibility if your presentation seems too polished. You don't want to appear to lecture people. Rather, you want to create the feeling of a one-on-one conversation with the audience.

In fact, Joyce vigorously discourages clients from memorizing an entire speech or presentation—because she's seen it have disastrous results. "I remember, in particular, one young man who worked for a well-known advertising agency. Every year this company gets together and their 'stars' from all over the world make team presentations of ad campaigns before a group of judges.

"Well, I could tell this fellow was taking these presentations entirely too seriously—he didn't realize that, in a way, it's all a game. So he was making himself crazy trying to memorize his remarks perfectly, and nothing I said could dissuade him. On the morning of his presentation, he got about twenty seconds into it and suddenly forgot what he was supposed to say next. Because he had memorized it word for word—rather than committing basic ideas to memory—his only option was to start over. He did, and this time he went maybe twenty-five seconds. Three times he started and stopped, and finally this young man, in front of the judges and in front of his peers, seemed to just melt. And he had to leave the stage. It was one of the worst moments I've ever experienced. I still get goose bumps when I remember it."

The moral of this story: Rather than rehearse to the point of perfection, simply practice your speech aloud several times. This technique can eliminate unnecessary blunders—awkward expressions, tongue twisters, and confusing homonyms, such as "site" and "sight"—and ensure that your speech's spoken length is appropriate. If your presentation involves visuals, be sure you know how and when to use them.

While this kind of simple practice is sufficient for many public speaking situations, if you expect to give speeches on a regular basis, you may want to go one step farther in your preparations, and record yourself. Or hire a professional coach to help you polish your presentation skills. When Joyce works with clients, she routinely videotapes them while they rehearse. Seeing yourself "live," as others see you, can reveal problems such as poor eye contact, bad posture, or nervous gestures—flipping your hair or constantly adjusting your tie, for example.

Even an ordinary tape recorder can be useful in learning how to pace your delivery and use your voice to support your message. For example, declarative statements should end on a falling inflection, advises Joyce. But many women just naturally end sentences on a rising inflection (which should be reserved for questions), and inadvertently create the impression they're tentative about what they're saying. Similarly, a sing-song rhythm sounds childlike.

To help you rate your voice, here's a list of questions Joyce uses with clients:
- ✔ Is my voice pleasant to listen to?
- ✔ Does my voice have any characteristics that I would consider undesirable in another speaker?
- ✔ Does my voice reflect what I intend to convey in thought and feeling?
- ✔ Were changes in pitch, loudness, duration, and tone quality appropriate to what I was saying?
- ✔ Would I listen to this voice if I were not the speaker?
- ✔ Does my voice reflect my personality?
- ✔ Did I get my message across?
- ✔ How can I improve the way I sound?

If you don't have access to a video camera or a tape recorder, rehearse in front of a full-length mirror. The point is to take a good hard look at yourself, as if you were in the audience. "Stepping outside yourself to study your performance isn't easy," says Joyce. "In this situation, most people have a difficult time finding something they like about themselves. Instead, they focus on their negative physical attributes.

"A good way to be more objective—and positive—is to make a list of five things you like about yourself. For example: being outgoing, energetic, knowledgeable. Make this list before your rehearsal," she advises. "Then, when analyzing your tape or watching yourself in the mirror, look first for these positive qualities."

Critiquing Your Speaking Style

Here are points to consider when evaluating speaking style:

Direct eye contact. Did you give the impression that you were looking at everyone? To make direct eye contact, talk to one person until you complete a point. Then move on to look at another person. "Visit" with each one from eight to ten seconds. And be sure to "work the room," making contact with all sections of the audience so everyone feels included.

Vocal energy and variety. Did you speak in short conversational sentences? Use punctuation marks as natural breathing points. Highlight key words in your notes as a reminder to emphasize them.

Gestures and facial expression. Did your hand and body movements add to your message—or simply distract the audience? Use your hands and arms to communicate ideas such as size, direction, emphasis, and number. Between gestures, remember to rest your hands at your sides or lightly on the lectern; keep them out of your pockets and away from your face and hair. Your facial expressions should reflect the tone of your message. Smile only when it's appropriate; smiling constantly will make you look insincere.

Fluency. Did your words flow smoothly? Have you avoided nonwords, such as "um," "uh," or "you know"? Substitute pauses for nonwords. Use silence as a bridge between different ideas—it gives your audience a chance to catch up with you and "digest" what you've said.

"Remember," advises Joyce, "you will be much harder on yourself than anyone else. By focusing on the positive, you will give yourself permission to say, 'I'm OK.' Feeling good about yourself will do a lot to enhance your overall performance while you work toward eliminating any characteristics that may distract from your message."

CONQUERING STAGE FRIGHT

Many people find that no matter how much effort they invest in advance preparation or how many times they've been on stage, they still get "butterflies" before every public appearance. Even professional performers—Johnny Carson, Barbara Streisand, Tom Selleck, and Bette Midler, to name a few—suffer bouts of stage fright. Midler, for one, freely admits that despite years of experience on stage and screen—she's done the cabaret route, won four Grammys, a Tony, several Emmys, and a couple of Oscar nominations—she still throws up before every show. "The only performers who don't get sick *are* sick," she maintains.

"Stage fright is a very normal reaction," Joyce says, "so don't make yourself 'wrong' for feeling the adrenaline. I remember one time when I was asked to pitch some business to clients who were my peers in the public relations business. And I did my presentation all right, but when I sat down my pulse was racing so fast I thought I was having a heart attack. I'd never been so nervous in my whole life, but it was understandable, because I cared so much about making a good impression on these people."

Although Kathy has come a long way in conquering her stage fright, she says, "I'm still intimidated by speaking in front of a group. That's why I always have a glass of water with me when I speak—so if I feel butterflies in my stomach, or my mouth starts to go dry, or my voice falters, I just nonchalantly take a sip of water.

"I remember once at a seminar called 'Take Control of Your Life and Start Your Own Business,' the speaker before me, *Working Woman* editor Adele Scheele told the group, 'Why do you think speakers have a glass of water up here—it's because we're nervous.' Later, when I gave my speech, just as I was starting to tell my story of overcoming shyness, I felt my voice start to go. So I picked up my glass of water and said, 'I think I'll take a drink now.' The audience roared," Kathy recalls, "and people told me later the audience 'was mine' after that moment. I think they identified with my feelings and suddenly the rapport was there."

The best way to handle stage fright is to "know it, expect it, welcome it," says Joyce. "For example, I get very cold before I speak to a large group. But instead of trying to get warm, I just say to myself, 'Here comes that cold feeling. That means all systems are go. You're charged, you're working, you care.' "

Other symptoms of stage fright include shortness of breath, sweaty palms, a dry mouth, and a panicky sensation that everything you know about your topic will suddenly drain from your brain. Relax. "The first thing you need to do," suggests Joyce, "is get out of the 'oh my God' syndrome: Oh my God, I'm going to blow it; oh my God, my mouth is going to go dry; oh my God, I'm going to lose my lunch. Because what happens is that those feelings become a negative, self-fulfilling prophecy. So change the tape in your head, and start giving yourself positive messages like, 'I'm ready to go. I know what I know.' "

Other things you can do to ease stage fright:

Take deep yoga-like breaths before going on stage and then try to place your voice where your breathing came from, advises Joyce. This not only calms you, it will prevent your first words from coming out in a high-pitched squeak. Yawning or laughing also work well to relieve tension.

Get moving, because physical activity will help release that feeling of tightness in your body. So walk over and check out the flip chart, for example. Or get a drink of water—almost any kind of movement will create an outlet for your nervous energy.

Personal Polish Tip

Plan a gesture as part of your opening statement. This will release adrenaline and get your system going the minute you begin your presentation.

Practice your opening again and again until you can say it in your sleep. This is the only part of a presentation you might want to memorize—because knowing you won't flub your first line gives you the added confidence you need to take the stage. "The moment you actually start your speech, you'll be fine," says Joyce. "Getting out of the starting gate is the toughest part."

Don't allow yourself to get distracted before you speak. "Very few speakers can answer a phone call or deal with some minor emergency before they speak, and not have it distract from their presentation," counsels the *Speaker's Idea File* newsletter. "Always take five minutes (or more) to collect your thoughts, focus on your message, and breathe before stepping up to the podium. Don't allow distractions to ruin what you've taken days to prepare."

Put the experience in perspective. "Think of your speech as the opportunity you always wanted to perform in public," says futurist Weiner. "I'm convinced that somewhere in every speaker's heart is the dream of being a rock star or even the host of *The Tonight Show*. When you're asked to give a talk, realize that this is probably the closest you'll ever get to the cabaret. It's a dream come true, the chance to captivate an audience. When you're through, you'll find yourself saying, 'Wow. If I can only do that again before I die...' "

COMMANDING THE PLATFORM
LIKE A PRO

You may recall that earlier we said the most successful speakers are adept at thinking on their feet. In other words, they manage to appear cool, calm, and collected, even when confronted with the unexpected. "Once when I was giving a speech," says Kathy, "I noticed a woman in the front row was sound asleep! (We'd just had a heavy lunch.) My former self would have taken that as rejection, but instead I focused on the rest of the group, who were eagerly listening to my every word. Look for the positive people in the group, because it increases your confidence."

But let's be realistic. You can't script every moment when you're dealing with the public. So we want to offer a few suggestions designed to help you gain and maintain control of your audience and your composure if you're confronted with the unexpected. Here are some typical unscripted moments, and suggestions for how to handle them:

When you need to take control of an audience that seems reluctant to settle down, make them anticipate the beginning of your presentation. You can do this simply by pausing for up to a minute after taking center stage. Use the time to adjust your notes, your stance, your glasses.

When you're pressed for time—because your part of the program has been trimmed, or another speaker ran long, or you simply can tell the audience is getting restless—present your most important points first. (Ideally, you'll have prioritized your thoughts when shaping your speech.) That way, if it's necessary to cut your speech short, you won't have sacrificed your message.

When someone interrupts what you're saying, don't try to ignore them. You can maintain control of the presentation by saying, "I'd like to respond to that, but first, I want to finish the point I was making."

When you're being questioned by someone who's obviously hostile, try this: Pause briefly to show you've given the question serious thought. Then respond with something like "You evidently have strong feelings about this," or "I respect your views— let me give you another perspective," suggests Roger

Ailes, a media consultant who's worked for both Ronald Reagan and George Bush. Whatever you say, Ailes advises, "never use the negative word 'but' to link your thoughts."

When you're asked a question that has been answered in your presentation, don't risk insulting the audience by saying, "I already covered that in my speech." Instead, offer a quick recap, then break eye contact with the person who asked the question to discourage further discussion on that particular point.

When you're asked a question you're not prepared to answer, don't hedge or try to fabricate information. The best way to stay out of trouble in this situation is to say something like, "That's too complicated for a brief answer," or "That's probably not of interest to everyone here, so why don't we talk about it later," or "Mr. Smith is our expert on that and I'd like to check with him so that I don't give you the wrong information. I will have the information for you by…"

THOUGH WE'VE PREACHED THE IMPORTANCE OF PREPARATION throughout this chapter, in closing, we'd like to share a story that illustrates one of the most valuable lessons you can learn about public speaking: expect the unexpected.

"I once was invited to give a presentation and the person who was to introduce me arrived drunk," recalls entrepreneur Barbara Winter. "Instead of telling the audience about me, she began a rambling account of her life story and sex life! Several members of the group tried to lure her off the stage, but she refused to leave. While the incident was uncomfortable, there was a hidden bonus in it all—the audience was both embarrassed and extremely sympathetic. I think I could have read from the telephone directory and they'd have cheered me on."

The moral of the story: "Be as prepared as possible," counsels Winter, "but be willing to laugh when things don't go as smoothly as you'd planned. You'll win more friends and influence more people if your approach is positive and flexible."

PART THREE

Assessing Your Life and Your Style

STYLE VS. SUBSTANCE:
Projecting an Image That Reveals the Real You

> *Diamonds are nothing more than chunks of coal that stuck to their jobs.*
> —Malcolm Forbes

> *Be not deceived with the first appearance of things, for show is not substance.*
> —English proverb

PERSONAL STYLE—PROJECTING AN IMAGE THAT REVEALS the real you—is something a lot of people struggle with, for good reason. To begin with, style is a composite of several skills, which makes it hard to define and thus potentially hard to master. Most of us instinctively sense style, but when we try to analyze why one person has it and another doesn't, the discussion invariably turns to things like fashion and physical attractiveness, concerns that are arguably superficial. Which is another reason style can be a tough topic: some people just don't put much stock in the notion. They argue "it's what's inside that really counts."

But there's considerable evidence to the contrary. Researchers have linked looks to earning power and promotions. For instance, university economists analyzing data from the United States and Canada found that attractive people earned more. It didn't matter whether the job was factory work or university teaching, better-looking employees made about 5 percent more per hour than people with average looks, while less attractive workers earned 5 to 10 percent below those with average looks.

While one might argue that a person can't really change their looks, many experts suggest there are ways to "package" yourself for success. Underestimating the power of a professional image can cost you opportunities, as Connie Brown Glaser and Barbara Steinberg Smalley demonstrate in their book *More Power To You!* The authors share the story of a Washington, DC, woman who, in her early thirties, after working ten years as an administrative assistant in a large accounting firm, applied for the position of office manager when her boss retired. But she wasn't even granted an interview!

Her reaction: "I thought it was just an oversight, so I asked the director of personnel what happened. He told me I didn't fit the image of an office manager. He suggested I revamp my wardrobe—get rid of my neon-colored skirts and dangling earrings—before I applied again for another position. I was shocked. I do a great job, and the way I dress shouldn't have any bearing. My clothes reflect my personal style." To which Glaser and Smalley conclude: "Forget about personal style."

While we won't go that far, we do think it's important to be aware of how you come across to others and to manage that perception to your best advantage. "One of my first bosses impressed this upon me—she always knew what image she wanted to portray and how she wanted to be perceived and treated," says Joyce. "I'll never forget something she told me one Saturday when we had to go into work because we were in the process of moving out of our offices. I had worn jeans and a sweatshirt, anticipating we would be packing and doing a lot of dirty work; she showed up wearing beautiful slacks and an elegant silk shirt, looking fabulous. So I asked her how she expected to work in those clothes. And she told me, 'You're dressed to move boxes; I'm dressed to supervise.' "

Like it or not, ours is a visual society and appearance is one of the first measures we use to size up a person's worth. As Jim Mullen and Hal Rubenstein observe in "Men's Fashions of the Times," a special issue of *The New York Times,* "What you choose to wear and how you choose to wear it reveals more personal data than a tax audit."

In this chapter, we'll focus on the relationship between style and substance: how the "outer you" can contribute to your success by helping people appreciate the "inner you." Personal style can be a great asset, if it helps you project an image that supports your goals. But, as the ambitious young woman in Washington learned too late, your style can just as easily betray you by sending subtle messages that contradict your intentions.

WHAT IS STYLE?

We all recognize style when we see it. Author Tom Wolfe with his signature double-breasted white suits and gentlemanly air has it. Another person who immediately comes to mind is Jacquelyn Kennedy Onassis. Her classic good looks and well-bred charm made this stately first lady the epitome of style for a whole generation. And the world eagerly watched Princess Di metamorphose from a cute kindergarten teacher to a regal beauty. You can probably name plenty of other examples, because a person with style has an unmistakable aura that sets them apart.

"Individual style is about doing your own thing, not someone else's," says image consultant Leah Feldon in her book *Dress Like A Million*. "It's taking bits and pieces of what's available and putting them together in your own personal way, breathing your own life into them."

Finishing Touches author Anne Oliver equates style with "packaging" and emphasizes the importance of perfecting "even the most minute detail...To get beyond the first impressions made on others, you must package yourself attractively but never forget that there must be something of value inside the package."

Even fashion mavens acknowledge the relationship between style and substance. Here's how the late designer Willi Smith put it: "Style is the person...People who have a great personal conviction about themselves and the way they want to look, look great...Style comes from within and is simply displayed on the exterior.' "

You can't buy style; it must be acquired. Many men and women just naturally discover their style in their early to mid-thirties as they become more clear and confident about who they are, the type of work they want to do, and the lives they aspire to lead. Others work at developing personal style, often turning to fashion and beauty consultants for guidance in defining or refining an image that reflects who they are—or hope to be.

Though discussions of style typically begin with personal appearance, our exploration won't end there, for style is as much a matter of attitude as attire. "Style is not fashion," observes writer Hal Rubenstein. "Clothes don't have style. You have style. Yes, you. You just may not know it. Because if you cook, own a home, travel by bike, car, or rollerblade, raise children, or worry about those who are dear to you, you exhibit style in other areas. You just haven't trained it on getting dressed. For style, true style, is the quality of imagination. It's the ability to place yourself in new situations with a fresh attitude and an eye on something better. You don't think you have that? Then what to wear is the least of your problems."

FASHIONING YOUR STYLE

Contrary to the familiar adage penned by the 19th-century philosopher Thomas Carlyle, clothes don't make the man—or woman—but they do add the finishing touches that are so critical to your image. "Think of clothes as accessories to your style. *You* want to be remembered, not *what* you're wearing—in other words, don't let your clothes wear you," advises Joyce, who routinely provides image consulting when helping clients prepare for public appearances.

Whether chosen carefully or haphazardly, a person's wardrobe speaks volumes about their taste, personal creativity, economic and professional status, and more. Style is that special knack of knowing which clothes and accessories will complement—and compliment—your body while expressing your individuality. Consider how personal style can influence the messages conveyed by a simple white T-shirt, observes Feldon: "By itself, it says 'everyman.' Roll up the sleeves and it says 'active and fashion savvy.' Iron it and it says 'neat and fastidious.' "

Dressing for Success: New Rules for the Nineties

Conventional wisdom has it that if you want to be considered a career climber, dress for your next step. "Men and women reaching for the top in business, politics, the arts, etc., know that in our visually oriented, competitive world, appearance transmits an immediate image that works for or against them," says image consultant Virginia A. Sullivan.

While there's no question that dressing the part of your ambitions is important, the formula dressing stressed in the eighties is now considered passé in many professional circles. As one Brooks Brothers' ad observes: "These days you never know. Is the sport coat a CEO or a new-minted MBA? Is that the software king in the baggy pants or a corporate VP in Friday trim? Success today is often out of uniform..."

Dressing for success in the nineties is not about adhering to rigid rules, but about knowing what makes you look and feel good. In all but the most buttoned-up businesses, dress codes are relaxing and many companies have even instituted "casual days" when employees are encouraged to forego formal office attire.

"This corporate casualness is a sign of changing times," according to *The Wall Street Journal*. "It reflects in part the rise of baby boomers—for whom blue jeans were once de rigueur—into positions of authority. Men may also be following the lead of the growing number of white-collar women, who many men feel have more flexibility in how they dress. Silicon Valley has also played a part, its higher profile lending legitimacy to its low-key look."

Style vs. Substance

As corporate America loses some of its stiffness, fashion-conscious men are taking advantage of these trends:

✔ Neckties are being abandoned in favor of mandarin-collar shirts, cashmere polos, and turtlenecks.(One upscale Manhattan boutique reports that tie sales have slipped 50 percent in the past three years.)

✔ Looser fitting designer suits in a variety of colors and textures are becoming as acceptable as the familiar dress blues or traditional pinstripes. In some offices, even a sport jacket paired with twill or khaki pants is considered suitable professional attire.

✔ The plain white shirt, though still widely favored, is no longer the only option for a well-dressed executive. Suits are being married with shirts bearing dynamic stripes or brighter, nontraditional shades, such as pink, turquoise, or cinnamon.

Even more dramatic is the revolution in women's work wardrobes. "When women marched into corporate offices in droves, they tended to imitate men's dress—a man-tailored shirt with a bow or pin at the neck," observes the newsletter *Office Hours.* "Now that women have taken their places in boardrooms, femininity has returned and individuality prevails." This perspective is supported by a *Working Woman* survey in which, of the more than 1,200 readers who responded, nearly 40 percent described their company's dress code as "anything goes"; fewer than 20 percent said they wore suits to work.

So what are professional woman wearing to work?

✔ Dresses now have equal status with suits—and many women prefer them for two reasons: they offer simple, one-step dressing and they're often more comfortable.

✔ Pants, especially in combination with a matching jacket, are favored by many female executives. Paired with a blouse or a chemise, pantsuits move easily from day to evening with a simple change of accessories.

✔ Choices in accessories have expanded. Bold jewelry, even sparkles, are considered quite chic for women working in the creative professions,

✔ The basic, dark colors once advocated for office wear are no longer the guiding rule. Today, a woman can pull off just about any shade, from pastel pink to emerald green, sunshine yellow to rich purple—as long as the style of her outfit is professional.

Dressing Strategies

Astute professionals recognize that every culture has its dress code, even if the rules aren't recorded in a policy manual. "When I worked for an entrepreneurial, casual-dress firm, I took the 'unofficial' dress code as seriously as when my paycheck came from a Fortune 500 monolith, because the informal dress code was as clear-cut as the other," says Martha H. Peak, an editor with the American

Management Association. "For similar reasons, I suspect that the folks at Microsoft choose their Dockers as carefully as IBMers pick their Big Blue suits."

Professional style depends on three things: your occupation, the region where you work and live, and your own sense of what flatters you. "Just as important as knowing what to wear is knowing when to wear it and having a reason for wearing it," counsels *Office Hours.* "Whatever you choose to wear to work, just remember that everything you put on makes a statement...whether that statement enhances your chances for advancement or hinders them is up to you."

Along that same line of thinking, *Working Woman* identified these "dressing strategies":

Aspirational Dressing. Dress for your next promotion and the position you want. For instance, if you want to be in management, dress the part. If you're a man and the male managers wear pinstripes, then you wear pinstripes. If the women wear skirted suits and dresses, you wear skirted suits and dresses.

Situational Dressing. Fit your clothes to the business at hand. For instance, if you know you're going to visit a construction site or production plant, skip the suit. A casual outfit, such as slacks and a sport shirt is much more appropriate. Situational dressing demands judgment—jeans and a T-shirt are too casual even for a plant visit.

Communicational Dressing. Instead of dressing for an occasion, dress for the company you'll be keeping. For example, you might feel out of place in a white

suit and pastel tie or scarf at a banker's convention—
but you'd fit right in at a gathering of art directors.

ARE YOU DUE FOR AN
IMAGE UPDATE?

Whatever dressing strategy you choose, most experts agree,
when you've got the "what to wear" question answered,
you can concentrate on getting the job done. "Above all,
clothes should make you feel good," says Joyce. "If you like
what you're wearing, you'll project an air of confidence—
and that's what style is really about."

But if you're like most people, you don't give your image
much thought until something happens to put you in the
spotlight. It could be a promotion or a presentation or an
important business trip. Suddenly you're racing out to buy
the perfect outfit and trying to squeeze into your schedule
your first haircut appointment in months. If this scenario
rings true, you're long overduc for an image update.

It's easy to get stuck in a kind of style time warp, says
Kathleen Walas, Avon's international beauty and fashion
director. "Both men and women, but especially women,
tend to stay within a certain look for themselves—whether
it's a hairstyle, or makeup, or type of clothing—that they
wore during the happiest time of their life. It could have
been when they just got married, or had children, or were
young and felt their most sexy. That's why you see many,
many women who are attractive, but they have a look that's
so dated, it's no longer flattering. For example, some
women will wear the same shade of lipstick for twenty or
thirty years.

"Obviously, this is something that happens unconsciously," Walas adds. "That's why both men and women need to make a concerted effort to assess their image every year or so."

Updating your image doesn't require a dramatic overhaul, just some periodic fine-tuning. Often the simplest changes can make a world of difference in how you're perceived. For instance, on the advice of fashion and beauty authorities, Princess Di began wearing shoulder pads that extended at least one inch beyond her natural shoulders—because it helped make her large waist look smaller.

Little Touches Mean A Lot

To give you a feel for the way style develops, we pulled together some real-life examples of how Joyce has helped clients rethink their images and how they package themselves. "I don't expect people to do a 360-degree turn," says Joyce. "But you'd be surprised how little touches can make a big difference in your image—without turning you into someone you're not comfortable being."

Here, from Joyce's experiences, are stories that illustrate some of the key touches that help shape style:

Professional accessories. "I had a client who was preparing to testify before a federal government hearing, so it was essential that he come across as an expert in his field. Overall, he was a nice-looking guy, except for one thing: he was carrying a briefcase that was so old and worn out, it was an embarrassing contradiction to our efforts to position him as a credible professional. So I said to him, 'Gee, I can tell that your briefcase has a lot of historical significance.' He took the hint and agreed to buy a new attaché case more in keeping with his image."

Personal grooming. "I was hired by a major accounting firm to work with a man who was being considered for promotion to partner. The only problem: he didn't look the part of an executive. His clothes were ripped and dirty. His tie had stains on it. His shoes weren't polished. And when he pulled his wallet from his pocket to give me his business card, there was food on it and a string dangling out of it. I didn't even want to take his card! Imagine the impression he was making on clients. As I explained to him, there's simply no excuse for not being neat and clean."

Finishing touches. "After one of my seminars on establishing a professional presence, a young woman from the audience came up and started telling me how her career seem to have stalled. That no matter how hard she tried, she couldn't seem to make much of an impression. In fact, people she'd been with in meetings and other professional settings sometimes didn't even remember her name. Well, I took one look at her and I could see why: from head to toe, she was brown. Her hair was a dull, mousy brown; her glasses were standard horn-rim frames; her dress was another shade of brown; and her nylons were tan. Even her earrings were small and nondescript. Earth tones are nice, but not if you blend into the background. Because she was an executive in a profession that values conservative dress, she didn't want to do anything too obvious to make herself stand out. So I suggested she spark up her image by adding a little color around her face. I recommended that she get red glasses and start wearing scarves and larger earrings that would frame her face (no dangling earrings, though!)"

Making A Fashion Statement

Style is such a personal expression, there's literally no end to the different looks that are possible—witty and whimsical, traditional and tailored, affluent or flashy, artistic or decidedly conservative, to name a few. But, as Elaine Louie, author of *The Manhattan Clothes Shopping Guide*, observes, "The look of success, whether it's avant-garde or conservative, usually is a look of polish."

To achieve true style, you must develop an eye for what looks good on you and then use that knowledge to build a wardrobe that lives up to the demands of the life you lead. Still struggling to discover a style that reveals the real you?

Steer clear of flamboyant fashion statements. A slavish acceptance of passing fads is often interpreted as the mark of someone who either lacks imagination or the self-confidence to be their own person.

Stick with classic shapes and styles if you want a versatile wardrobe that affords long-lasting good looks. "Don't confuse classic with conservative," cautions Walas. For example, jeans are a classic style, but bell-bottoms are a fad. Other examples of classics: tweed blazers; turtlenecks; wool slacks; loafers; a trench coat; a crisp, white shirt or silk blouse.

Opt for quality over quantity, and concentrate on building a foundation of basics you can wear year after year. Most image consultants recommend investing in at least one major piece per season. It could be a new coat or a great pair of boots or that designer attaché case you've been coveting.

Give your wardrobe an up-to-the-minute attitude by adding a trendy touch or two, such as an item in the season's hottest color or fabric. Shoes, ties or scarves, vests, and hats are some of the easiest and least expensive ways to spice up your basic wardrobe.

Pay attention to flattering feedback. If you always get compliments or people ask if you've lost weight when you wear a particular outfit, chances are the style or color, or both, compliment you.

Favor "season-less" fabrics if you want to get the most mileage out of your wardrobe. A good lightweight wool, for instance, can be worn all year. Also, avoid mystery fabrics with creative names like Belgian linen and French cotton. A much better choice: classic blends and natural fibers, such as tweeds, soft flannel, gabardine, and silk.

For Men Only...

How much you spend on clothes isn't as important as how they fit. This is especially true of shirts and suits, which should conform to your frame without bumps or ripples. Be sure jacket lapels don't bow—that's a sure sign there's not enough room in the chest and shoulder area.

Ties with large patterns tend to draw attention to themselves, and not you. Subtle and symmetrical patterns with no more than four colors are the most versatile choice, especially if your work requires you to operate in a variety of settings and business cultures.

For Women Only...

Because women's fashion traditionally has been innovative, their clothing decisions are considerably more complex. "Women reinvent themselves every day," observes William Grimes, a culture reporter for *The New York Times*. "And they face an intimidatingly large field of choices. Consider the skirt (if, in fact, it's going to be a skirt and not slacks, or leggings with some sort of loose outer garment, or those culotte things that look like a skirt.) It can hit at the shoe, the ankle, midcalf, just below the knee, just above the knee, or onward and upward to the midthigh. The look can be mannish, mannish-womanish, womanish-mannish, boyish, girlish, or androgynous. It can quote (wittily or seriously) a Navy uniform, Russian peasant garb, a Matisse painting, 1930s Hollywood glamour portraits by Hurell, a dandy or any combination of the above.

"That's not the end of it, either. Shoes, earrings, bracelets, scarves, and purses can make or break a look," he continues. "When the alarm clock goes off, it's a miracle that modern woman does not simply lie there, stunned, and curse her fate."

If you're caught in the kind of fashion quandary Grimes describes, here are some ways to streamline your morning routine without skimping on style:

Dare to be arbitrary. Rather than filling your closet with a rainbow of colors, pick a palette you're comfortable with and stick to it. This may sound restrictive at first, but it's actually freeing because it simplifies your clothing choices. Start with a base color that's neutral, and thus trend resistant, and build your wardrobe around it.

For example, suggests Feldon, if you're partial to earth tones, which work especially well if you have auburn hair, you might pick brown as your base color for slacks or skirts, and then add shirts or blouses and accessories in rust, beige, olive, and khaki. Other flattering combinations: Pale blondes might consider the beiges (from ivory to taupe to greige), aubergine, or navy. Redheads and strawberry blondes almost always look great in slate blue, charcoal gray, and dusty sage. Black, navy, and white are best bets for dark brunettes or olive-skinned women. If you're not sure which palette would work best for you, don't hesitate to get your colors done by a professional—a little expert advice can help you avoid a lot of mistakes.

Personal Polish Tip

Extreme color contrasts tend to visually break up the body, so if you want to look slimmer, stick to one all-over color or at least mix colors of the same value.

Invest in separates that can be mixed and matched. Many professionals pare their wardrobe to a handful of key pieces—usually four to eight blazers and slacks or skirts—which they artfully rotate, creating an infinite variety of looks with the help of well-chosen accessories.

Personal Polish Tip

Avoid jewelry that makes noise—bracelets that clack when you move and earrings that dangle and jingle. Also, pick jewelry that's proportionate to your frame. "If you're petite and small-boned beware of too-big or too-bold necklaces, earrings, and scarves that may overwhelm you," advises Walas. "Big boned? You can carry off bolder accessories, big square-cut scarves, larger pins, dramatic necklaces and earrings. Tiny pieces of jewelry will get 'lost' on you."

Buy entire outfits by a designer to look pulled together with minimal effort. Or create your own tried-and-true, no-thinking-required combos, right down to matching shoes and bag.

Develop your own "uniform dressing," suggests Feldon, by settling on a limited number of styles, lines, and colors that are suited to your body, personality, and lifestyle. "Lean-line pants, a simple cardigan, and ballet-slippers, for instance, is a silhouette that could work well for a slim Audrey Hepburn type who worked in the arts. Short skirts, T-shirts, and unstructured jackets could form a winning uniform foundation for a TV producer (with good legs). Long skirts, large, belted overblouses, and jackets might be a great everyday look for a full-figured saleswoman."

Personal Polish Tip

"If you're bothered by static cling, rub a small amount of hand cream on your palms, then glide them over your pantyhose," suggests Kathy. The static cling will disappear!

Choose shoes with a slightly raised heel. Because this style works equally well with skirts and pants, you'll need fewer pairs to build a versatile but functional shoe wardrobe. Black, navy, and taupe are smart picks, especially for professional women. To round out your footwear, you might splurge on a pair of "fun shoes" in red, blue, or another bright color.

Personal Polish Tip

Think twice about wearing sneakers—even on the street—when you're working. This is a lesson Joyce learned the hard way early in her career when she unexpectedly ran into a client she very much wanted to impress. "He looked me over from head to toe, saw my sneakers and said, 'Are you having fun?' At that moment, I made a decision to stop wearing high heels and buy only shoes I could wear all day and even run through airports with, while still looking professional."

Effortless dressing begins with planning. Paying attention to your wardrobe won't give you immediate results, but one day in the near future, you'll be surprised when you open your closet and find that it doesn't take forever to figure out what to wear.

Professional Grooming

It's almost impossible to look pulled together if you haven't attended to your personal grooming with the same care you've given to your clothing. Remember, style is in the details. To ensure you always look your best:

Get regular haircuts. Men, and women with short styles, should visit the barber or stylist every six weeks. Shampoo often, and if you color your hair, watch those roots—because you never want anyone else to see them. Likewise, if you wear a beard or mustache, be meticulous about keeping it trimmed.

Treat yourself to a manicure at least once a month. Businesspeople's hands are always on display—when brochures are offered, products shown, contracts signed. If you don't have access to a professional manicurist, learn to give yourself a manicure at home. Regardless of gender, nails should be trimmed fairly short and cuticles pushed back. If you want to wear polish, a subtle shade is your best choice; because you don't have to worry about it clashing with your outfit and chips are less likely to show.

Wear fragrance judiciously. You don't want your aftershave or perfume entering the room before you do and lingering long after you leave.

Personal Polish Tip

Keep eyedrops and breath mints handy, in your purse or briefcase. Both are great refreshers when you're on the run.

Making the Most of Makeup

Women today have a whole new attitude about beauty: They believe inner beauty, good health, and good skin are every bit as important as wearing the right makeup. Accompanying this more confident attitude is a trend toward lighter and more neutral makeup, and an emphasis on creating a polished look with fewer products.

We favor this less-is-more approach because it's

- *quick and easy.* "I learned a long time ago that I could spend two hours getting ready or I could do it in fifteen minutes—and in the end, it didn't make much difference in how I looked," says Joyce. "Practically speaking, most working women can't spare much time in the morning for their beauty routine." Kathy adds: "When I'm *really* rushed, I can be out the door in as little as two minutes, using four basic items—pressed powder, blush, mascara, and lipstick—and know that I won't be embarrassed if I run into someone I know!"

- *flattering.* Stronger shades demand not only a good eye for color but a deft hand during application—otherwise, you look "made-up."

> ## Personal Polish Tip
>
> When using makeup, remember that light and frosted colors bring forth a feature and maximize it, advises Kathy. Dark, matte colors push back and minimize. If you don't know what your best facial feature is, ask a pro to help you figure out if it's your eyes, or beautiful skin, or whatever, and have them show you how to play it up. "So many women could be more attractive with a little bit of help, but they're afraid to ask!"

Because decisions about makeup depend on so many variables—your complexion, your age, your professional surroundings—it would be foolhardy to offer specific advice here. But we would like to share this simple ten-step, ten-minute makeup routine that you can adapt to your own beauty needs:

1. Brighten and cleanse your face with a toner. (This assumes you've thoroughly cleansed your face the night before.)
2. If your skin is dry, apply moisturizer after the toner. Opt for a moisturizer with a sunscreen, at least an SPF 15.
3. Once moisturizer is absorbed, apply cream foundation in a circular motion, either with your fingers or a cosmetic sponge, whichever you prefer. Don't forget your eyelids—foundation helps eyeshadow stay on longer.
4. Apply soft eyeliner to the upper eyelid. Eyeliner on the lower lid is generally aging and underscores faults such as lines or bags.

225

5. Follow with a dark taupe eyeshadow all over the eyelid, then put a lighter taupe shadow under the brow. Blend the two carefully. (You can use other colors of eyeshadow, but these two shades generally are easiest to work with.)

6. If needed, apply blush. Brush on two shades of rosy-hued blusher. Don't contour—use one shade over the other for depth. For a sun-kissed look, use a full brush to lightly dust temples, chin, and neck, as well as cheeks, with blush.

7. If a matte finish is desired, dust on transparent powder.

8. Brush your brows, and if necessary, use an eyebrow pencil or brow thickener to even out color and shape.

9. Apply mascara; two light coats are better than one heavy coat. You may want to precede the mascara with a lash conditioner.

10. Apply your lipstick, then outline lips with a matching lip pencil. Doing it in this order ensures a more natural look. To make lipstick last for hours, try this trick: Use the lip pencil to completely cover your lips. Then apply your lipstick. Blot, and apply a second coat of lipstick.

Personal Polish Tip

Once you've finished applying your makeup, always check it a minute to two later—or just before you leave the house, suggests Kathy. "This is the time to make sure your mascara hasn't smudged and that everything is blended smoothly. Cotton swabs and foam cosmetic wedges are my favorite tools for correcting makeup mishaps."

Seeking Expert Advice

Most of us find it difficult to step outside ourselves and be objective about our looks. If you're not sure about how to make the most of your strengths or you need an image update, consider turning to a professional.

Image consultants typically offer the most comprehensive approach and charge a fee for their services. A good image consultant will deal with your whole "package," offering advice on everything from hair color and the cut of jacket that's most flattering for your frame, to suggestions on how to carry yourself so you project the proper image in professional situations.

You also may want to take advantage of the free advice that's available from various retailers. For example, many hair salons offer consultations on style and color as a courtesy to prospective customers. Some even feature makeup application and lessons as part of their makeover services. Another great place to get a mini-makeover: cosmetic counters at major department stores.

Likewise, most major clothing stores are staffed with personal shoppers who can help you build a wardrobe within your allotted budget. Usually there's no minimum purchase required, and if you call ahead to let them know what you need, they'll often do some preliminary searching.

Even regular salespeople can be a good resource. For example, we know of one fellow who began to rethink his whole look after a salesman at an eyeglass shop suggested the horn-rim frames he was accustomed to wearing actually overshadowed his small features and seemed to hide his attractive blue eyes. Up until then, this fellow hadn't paid much attention to his features; today he's outfitted with a wardrobe of eye-catching designer frames—one of several touches that give him a distinctive style.

Don't be shy about soliciting the opinions of fashion and beauty consultants. After all, you don't have to follow their advice verbatim—just pick the best ideas and forget the rest. "Nobody is ever going to completely make you into who you think you really want to be," counsels Walas. "But you should walk away from every encounter with new techniques, insights, and tips that you can put together to create a terrific look you're comfortable with, and that you can recreate yourself."

LOOKING GOOD FROM THE INSIDE OUT

While any discussion of style naturally begins with personal appearance, it shouldn't stop there, because true style works from the inside out. Feeling fit is fundamental to looking good. And we're not just talking about shapely calves or enviable biceps. A healthy outlook also can work wonders for your image—it's been said that of all the things you wear, your expression is the most important.

In today's hurried world, many people feel they don't have time to take care of themselves the way they'd like to. "There's no question that Americans are experiencing more stress than ever," says Dr. Paul Rosch, president of the American Institute of Stress. One problem, he says, is techno-stress. "A variety of technological enhancements have put a premium on quantity instead of quality. We live in a sped-up society. With fax machines, it's now possible to contact almost anyone in the world at anytime. We suffer from information overload."

The busier we are, the more burdensome it becomes to do those things that give us a sense of well-being—like finding the time to exercise, making the effort to eat right, getting enough rest, and engaging in relaxing activities that nourish the spirit. But the benefits of regularly "recharging your batteries" can't be overemphasized. We recently read, for instance, about a study which found that people who were believed to be suffering from depression were, in fact, struggling with sheer exhaustion.

Increasingly, the medical profession and health experts are giving greater credence to the holistic view, long held by many cultures, that the mind and body are irrevocably linked, that illness can be brought on not only by external forces, but by one's state of mind. Simply put, stress seems to weaken the immune system and happiness to strengthen it. And there are many studies indicating that meditation, yoga, and other mind-body therapies can help reduce pain, lower cholesterol levels, ease symptoms of illness, and curb the physiological and psychological impact of stress.

Just as you periodically assess your wardrobe, it's wise to take stock of your well being from time to time. Do you feel good about who you are? Are you as healthy as you could be? Do you feel in control of your life? Are you proud of the way you look when you leave the house in the morning or do you dread getting dressed because the waistband on your slacks or skirt seems to get tighter every time you put it on?

Do you bounce out of bed, or do you drag yourself to the shower, dreading the start of another day because you're simply going through the motions of your professional and personal life? Though some people just naturally seem to have the stamina and spirit to constantly push ahead, most of us have to work at it.

Here's how talk show dynamo Sally Jessy Raphael gets going every morning: "While I'm exercising the body, I'm exercising my mind. So I start my day with an upbeat tape such as *Thinking Big*, or another one called *Chop Wood, Carry Water*, done by Richard Thomas—John Boy of *The Waltons*," she says in her autobiography, *Sally: Unconventional Success*. We share this example because Raphael has hit on one of the most critical elements of style: balance.

How Self-Image Shapes Style

Have you ever noticed how happy, confident, dynamic individuals just naturally strike you as attractive? In truth, their appeal has less to do with physical features or fashion statements than how they feel about themselves. "Psychologists emphasize that the way you view yourself can determine what you project to others," explains Walas.

Sadly, when it comes to self-image, most of us short-change ourselves. Conditioned from an early age to hold ourselves up to unrealistic standards established by the media, we bemoan real and imagined physical flaws instead of appreciating the qualities that make us unique. "If you feel you're too tall," cautions Walas, "you'll probably tend to slump a little, and others will pick up on it. But if you view yourself positively, if you truly believe that you're attractive, you'll feel better about yourself in general and project that impression to friends and acquaintances."

One method Walas suggests for improving your self-image: "Start by standing in front of a mirror and really 'seeing' yourself for the first time. Look for your assets—curly hair; clear, glowing skin; big, expressive eyes; or a smile that lights up your face. Everyone is special in some way."

Developing A Healthy Outlook

By nature, we humans tend to take a pessimistic view of life. Instead of focusing on life's joyful, uplifting moments, we dwell on disturbing experiences or painful topics. This response is partly biological. According to psychologists, negative sensations represent possible threats to our survival, so we're genetically programmed to view them as more urgent than positive feelings.

But habit also plays a role in our outlook, contends Dr. Herbert Benson, author of *Your Maximum Mind*. The more we dwell on the unpleasant ideas that ramble through our minds, the more deeply ingrained this pattern of thinking becomes. Eventually, Benson maintains, we effectively etch physical circuits of pessimism in our brains, so that our thoughts automatically turn in a downbeat direction.

You can open your mind and increase your potential for joy by evoking what Benson calls the "relaxation response." It's a simple technique that begins with morning meditation. Sit for a few minutes with your eyes closed and muscles relaxed as you breathe slowly in and out. With each exhalation, repeat a focus word or words, such as "shalom," "peace," or "let go." Dismiss any stray thoughts. After about ten minutes, your brain will be extremely receptive to new ideas and you can stimulate it with uplifting messages that, over time, will change your outlook.

While some researchers believe our ability to be optimistic is formed during childhood, Walas points out, others maintain that your optimism level can change over the years, depending on what's happening in your life, on the types of people you work with and socialize with, and on the ways you motivate yourself.

In her book *Real Beauty...Real Women*, Walas outlines ten steps for redirecting your thinking toward the positive. Among them:

Start by teaching yourself to view problems as challenges that offer you the opportunity to discover a creative solution and learn from your actions. Begin with smaller challenges: for example, if your ten-year-old's report card is full of more C-minus than B-plus grades, rather than chalking it up to "just one more thing I have to deal with!" view the report as signaling an opportunity to sit down with your child to formulate a better study plan (and, perhaps, to spend more time with him), as well as prompting a meeting with his teacher so you can work together on your child's behalf.

Consciously set goals at home, at work, in your community activities. If you feel shy about taking risks, start with small goals you're 90 percent sure you'll succeed at (for instance, acting as *one* of the coordinators of your church or temple's annual rummage sale or fund drive). As you reach each goal, set new ones. You'll find yourself striving to meet larger, more difficult challenges (and you'll experience increased self-confidence).

Keep a "win list" in your wallet or a desk drawer. On a 3-by-5-inch card, jot down all the things you like about yourself, plus the times you've succeeded with flying colors. Go over the list every day (or, at the very least, when you're feeling down). By affirming your worth, you'll feel good about yourself.

Do a periodic attitude check. During the afternoon, take five minutes to ask yourself, "How am I doing, feeling, today? Am I approaching this particular task positively or negatively?" If you're feeling angry, a little depressed, or just plain overwhelmed, try to get away for ten minutes or twenty minutes.

Give Yourself A Break

You can't hope to achieve the sense of well-being that's so essential to style when you're wrung out from the demands of your life. Yet many professionals seem to have become addicted to nonstop schedules, thriving on the stress that's involved. "Like a hostage enthralled by her captors, I have come to love my stress," science writer Dava Sobel says in an article for *Working Woman.* "Stress pervades my life, jolts my nervous system at each new crisis and often gives me a positive rush of energy that feels illicit in its power. I harbor no fantasies of a stress-free existence. It wouldn't suit me at all."

As a society, we have begun to recognize the toll that stress takes on our bodies and the impact it has on our quality of life. The only antidote is relaxation—"a concept foreign to most professionals," Sobel notes. "True workaholics and stress junkies don't even understand the meaning of the word."

Stress Check-Up

Here's a quick quiz to help you recognize the damaging effects of stress. Check each description that applies. Are you

experiencing colds or other minor infections
more often than in the past? ❑

frequently exhausted, even when you are getting
enough sleep and little or no physical exercise? ❑

working harder and longer without making
satisfactory progress? ❑

regularly feeling guilty when you leave uncom-
pleted work, even after putting in a full day? ❑

worrying a great deal about the future and too
often attempting to second-guess your supervisor? ❑

feeling insecure or fearful about tasks or
responsibilities you previously handled with ease? ❑

regularly questioning the motives of others,
perhaps even friends with whom you have
had long and pleasant associations? ❑

having frequent confrontations with people,
either on the job or at home? ❑

having increasing trouble making decisions,
perhaps even small, unimportant ones? ❑

finding that insignificant disappointments or
setbacks make you unduly depressed or angry? ❑

If you checked *five or more* items, you may be suffering from too much stress, according to Dr. Martin C. Sampson, president of the executive search firm Sampson, Neil & Wilkins. While stress can be debilitating, it doesn't have to be—there are many simple, common sense practices for confronting and controlling it.

Here, from Dr. Sampson and other health experts, are a dozen ways you can bust stress while boosting your physical and mental energy:

STRESS BUSTER #1
Exercise Regularly

Although exercise is often the first thing to go when our lives become frenzied, it must be considered as much a necessity for good health as eating and sleeping. So start penciling thirty-minute exercise sessions into your calendar. Most health experts recommend aerobic activities, but that doesn't mean your workout has to be an endurance test. For instance, a half hour of vigorous walking (covering roughly one mile in fifteen minutes) three times a week has been shown to reduce the risk of heart attack, stroke, diabetes, and even cancer by 55 percent. If you can't spare thirty minutes, aim for ten-minute breaks; new research indicates that several short but brisk breaks per day, such as climbing stairs, can produce the same health benefits as one long workout.

STRESS BUSTER #2
Set Aside Some Private Time Every Day

Some experts suggest devoting as much as ninety minutes daily to pure relaxation. You might listen to soft music or read something you enjoy; others find it helpful to listen to motivational tapes. And if life's really getting you down, take a break from your worries by watching an upbeat movie.

STRESS BUSTER #3
Eat a Healthy Diet

Here's what Walas recommends: "By getting the right amounts of carbohydrates, proteins, vitamins, minerals (especially vitamins C and A, which are depleted during stressful times, and iron, a must for energy), you can not only keep your energy high, you'll also help minimize your risk of colds and flu. What's more, three meals a day (with healthy between-meal snacks) will keep your blood sugar on an even keel, and you'll avoid the blahs, blues, and fatigue that can accompany a sudden dip in blood sugar."

STRESS BUSTER #4
Explore Relaxation Techniques

Research shows that practicing stress-reduction techniques such as biofeedback, meditation, stretching, deep breathing, and visualization regularly—say a half hour each day—can help pressured professionals improve their efficiency and productivity, not to mention the length and quality of their lives.

STRESS BUSTER #5
Develop a Hobby or Outside Interest

Rewarding yourself with an activity you enjoy, whether it's gardening, playing golf, baking, practicing a musical instrument, or sewing can help boost your energy, and make you feel better all the way around.

STRESS BUSTER #6
Keep a Journal

"New studies suggest that people who are able to write about their innermost feelings may enjoy better mental and physical health," says Walas. "Writing is also a powerful tool that helps you to organize overwhelming events and make them more manageable." Don't be discouraged if your first efforts focus on daily events—most people quickly transition to a more reflective mode.

STRESS BUSTER #7
Take Time Off

At least once a month plan a weekend free of work, and schedule longer vacations at least once a year. In a national survey of five hundred executives conducted by Hyatt Hotels and Resorts, three out of four respondents noted that vacations improved their job performance; nine out of ten deemed them a necessity for combating job-related stress.

STRESS BUSTER #8
Forget Your Own Worries by Helping Others

Donate your time and talents to charitable organizations, or send an uplifting card to a sick friend, or schedule an hour a week to help an illiterate adult learn to read. There are any number of volunteer activities you can choose from. The most important thing is to devote your time and energies to focusing on someone else's needs.

STRESS BUSTER #9
Pamper Yourself

The simple act of soaking in the tub for fifteen minutes, especially when the experience is accompanied by fragrant oils and soothing music, can rejuvenate body and soul. Or treat yourself to a facial, manicure, pedicure, or massage.

STRESS BUSTER #10
Schedule "Worry Time"

Some people find that being allowed to worry occasionally for a few minutes can actually help them cope better. The trick is to limit your worrying to the scheduled session. If troublesome thoughts pop into your head at other times, simply write them down for later reflection and go back to what you're doing.

STRESS BUSTER #11
Laugh—or Cry

Both reactions provide physiological relief from tension, anxiety, and emotional pain. When you laugh, you increase your heart rate, stimulate circulation, exercise your diaphragm, abdominal wall, and other muscles; equally important, laughter increases the production of certain hormones that serve as the body's natural painkillers. Similarly, the tears you produce when you're upset contain stress-relieving hormones. (The same hormonal effect is not achieved if your eyes water because of irritation.)

STRESS BUSTER #12
Take a Nap

A well-timed catnap can energize you and actually improve your stamina and judgment. The key to quality napping: Start before extreme fatigue sets in and don't overdo the dozing. A nap should last at least twenty minutes, or you'll awaken more tired than before, but no more than sixty minutes, or you run the risk of waking up in a stupor that some experts call "sleep inertia."

DEVELOPING YOUR OWN PERSONAL STYLE TAKES TIME and practice, and you may have to "try on" a variety of images before you discover the one that reveals the real you, that gives you the polish you need to succeed.

Personal style is one of those things that can give you an extra edge when competing for opportunities like a new job, a promotion, or, if you're an entrepreneur, new business. And for that reason alone, no aspiring professional can afford to dismiss style as mere superficiality. At the same time, the importance of style shouldn't be overestimated, for without substance—the attitude, skills, and goals necessary for success—style truly is nothing more than fancy packaging.

Chapter 11

STOP THE CLOCK:
Managing Your Time and Your Life

> *You can't have everything.*
> *Where would you put it?*
> —Steven Wright, comedian

> *To do great important tasks,*
> *two things are necessary:*
> *a plan and not quite enough time.*
> —Anonymous

"IF YOU WANT SOMETHING DONE, GIVE THE JOB TO A BUSY person," goes a familiar adage. And it does seem to be true that the more responsibility a person shoulders, the more capable they become at juggling a variety of tasks. Often pressure has a way of forcing us to become clearheaded about priorities. Suddenly, things that seemed so important yesterday fall away in the face of new demands and deadlines. Any major life change—a new job, the arrival of a child, a decision to go to college, sudden illness in the family—can force us to step back and reevaluate. As problems and priorities change throughout our lives, so do choices

241

about where to invest our time and energies. Just ask any new mother who's facing the challenge of returning to work. Everything from her morning beauty routine to the way she uses her lunch hour is bound to change.

On a larger scale, our society's notion of time—its value and how it should be spent—seems to be changing. You can see this simply by browsing the time management section of your local bookstore. If titles such as *Streamlining Your Life: A 5-Point Plan for Uncomplicated Living; Balancing Acts; Slow Down...And Get More Done;* and *You Don't Have To Go Home From Work Exhausted!* are any indication of the national mind-set, we're starting to ask whether it's possible to have lives that are full but not constantly frantic. While in the eighties our society put a premium on packing every minute of every day with appointments and activities, there seems to a general shift in the nineties toward a slower pace, inspired by the realization that living life in a dead run is not the road to lasting satisfaction.

"Leisure time, not money, is the status symbol of the nineties," says University of Maryland sociology professor John Robinson. In a study conducted for Hilton Hotels, Robinson found that 70 percent of Americans making $30,000 a year or more would like to give up a day's pay each week for one or two days off. Nearly a third of those polled were worried that they didn't spend enough time with family and friends.

"Everybody is trying to work fewer hours," says Lesley Friedman, president of a firm that places lawyers in temporary jobs. "People tell me, 'I'll give up my $150,000 salary if I can lead a more balanced life.' "

As part of this changing perspective, the notion of "superwoman" is being scorned, or at the very least, viewed with increased skepticism—especially by the generation of women who tried to live up to that model. Witness this counsel from a quiz in *Working Woman:* "'Having it all' is a meaningless goal that launches people on a frenetic, insatiable quest for more without the time to enjoy the process or savor the rewards. Women's desire to have it all stems partly from the mistaken notion that men traditionally have had it all; instead, men have sacrificed time with their children to shoulder primary financial responsibility for their families."

As more and more families find it necessary to have two incomes, couples are managing their lives differently. Many women no longer feel compelled to prove they can juggle the dual roles of happy homemaker and fast-track career climber; instead, they're looking to their husbands and children for support with household chores and family responsibilities, even if it means forfeiting their fantasies of picture-perfect lives. At the same time, many more men are coming to terms with what it means to truly shoulder their fair share in family life.

For one reason or another, it seems everyone struggles with stress and the frustration of always feeling rushed, overworked, and clearly over committed in the sense that they can't possibly do everything they *need to do* and still find time for the things they *want to do.* In his book *Timelock: How Life Got So Hectic and What You Can Do About It,* author Ralph Keyes equates the time pressures people feel today with "gridlock," the term engineers use when traffic has grown so congested that it can no longer move. "Timelock is the condition that occurs when claims on our time have grown so demanding that we feel it's impossible to wring one more second out of a crowded calendar," Keyes writes.

As part of his research, Keyes asked 443 people to fill out a questionnaire about time. More than half—66 percent—felt their lives had grown busier in the past year. Likewise, more than half agreed with the statement, "There aren't enough hours in the day to do everything I have to do." And 31 percent felt that "on the whole I have just about enough time to do what I have to do." In short, Keyes found that 85 percent of the people he studied felt they had virtually no "spare" time. Among the responses he cites as typical is the Minneapolis businesswoman who said, "You prioritize, list your 'musts,' then you can't even get to your musts."

Many books have been written on time management by experts who've devoted years to this field of study, so clearly there's no single way to win the clock race we all run. But on this the experts agree: the race is worth running. As management guru Peter Drucker observes, "Time is the scarcest resource and unless it is managed, nothing else can be managed."

Our goal here is to share some of the current thinking and innovative insights on time management, as well as a few tried-and-true tips, especially as they relate to the idea of selling yourself. Because just as a new outfit can add a special spring to your step, the ability to effectively manage your time and take control of your life can reduce the pressures and stress that drain your energy, threaten your peace of mind, and prevent you from projecting a competent, confident image.

THE MYTH OF THE FORTY-HOUR WEEK

If you put off more today than you can ever accomplish tomorrow, exhaust yourself by 4 P.M. with only a fraction of your work done, never get around to making decisions, dread the phone ringing, or the next business meeting, you may have fallen for "the myth of the forty-hour week." The truth is, many people in business today routinely put in ten-hour days, plus time on the weekends.

A survey by The Executive Committee, a San Diego–based organization of CEOs and company presidents, found in a nationwide poll of 505 CEOs (474 males and 31 females) that 40 percent routinely work between fifty and fifty-nine hours per week and 32 percent typically work sixty to sixty-nine hours.

Similarly, a Harris Poll found that free time has fallen nearly 40 percent in the last two decades. This isn't surprising, when you realize that during that same time period, the number of hours the average American worked in a year increased by 138 percent. This time squeeze is felt most keenly by women, says Harvard University professor Juliet B. Schor in her book *The Overworked American: The Unexpected Decline of Leisure*. Comparing annual hours of paid employment in all industries and occupations during the past twenty years, Schor estimates, "Men are working nearly a hundred more hours per year—or an extra two-and-a-half weeks—while women are putting in about three hundred additional hours—which translates into an extra seven-and-a-half weeks."

The obvious danger of the forty-hour week myth is that you can easily overextend yourself. Adding another meeting here and there (you tell yourself it's only an hour) can suddenly put you in overload if you're already underestimating your current commitments—which is pretty common.

Assessing Your Commitments

Most people spend their time with little thought of where it goes. Yet one of the first principles of effective time management is accurately assessing your commitments and appreciating the time each one takes.

That's why it's a good idea to periodically step back and take a hard look at where you're investing your attention and energy. More importantly, especially if you're feeling "timelocked," you need to evaluate your activities in terms of what you want to get out of life—not simply how much you can get done.

"You can create change in your life by altering the percentage of time you give to various commitments," advises Judith M. Bardwick, author of *The Plateauing Trap: How to Avoid it in Your Career and Your Life.* The reason: "Roughly speaking, your psychological commitment is proportionate to the amount of time you give to something. For many, time is a very scarce commodity; when you give time, you give something that is very valuable to you and therefore to the recipient of it."

Here's an exercise to help you determine if you're getting a good return on your investment. Keep track of your 168 hours per week, then fill out the following time card by calculating the percentage of time you give to

_____ work (include commuting time)

_____ sleep

_____ your spouse or lover, without the children

_____ your children, without your spouse or lover

_____ the family as a whole

_____ reading that is unrelated to work

_____ hobbies

_____ the arts

_____ athletics

_____ the community
_____ friends
_____ yourself

Once you've figured out where your time and energy is really spent, fill out the time card again—this time as you would like your life to be. Using this as your guide, you can start making adjustments to achieve a more balanced life.

SCHEDULING YOURSELF FOR SUCCESS

Do you control your work day or does it control you? Are your best intentions to be productive sabotaged by an over-flowing in-basket, countless phone calls, and a steady stream of drop-in visitors? If you never seem to get caught up, let alone get to your long-term goals, chances are you're letting other people decide the course of your day. Clearly it's time to try a new approach.

Spend Time On The Right Things

Rather than advocating techniques for increased efficiency, time management guru Edwin Bliss encourages people to focus their energies on the right things. So how do you know what those are? The first step, says Bliss, author of *Getting Things Done: The ABCs of Time Management,* is to write down all your goals. Then go through the list and delete everything except those you are *truly willing to work for.*

Don't be too quick to discount this deceptively simple advice—coming to terms with your dreams for tomorrow is essential if you want to make today more productive. Many people confuse staying busy with actually being productive. They're easily detoured from their own priorities because they spend their time reacting and responding to pressures from other people or things.

Success requires focus, so start each day by identifying the single most *important* thing you want to accomplish, no matter what. Important tasks are the ones with the greatest long-term payoff—and not necessarily the most *urgent* ones. Next, schedule a block of time to devote to the task you've identified; your other responsibilities should be scheduled around this block, in order of importance.

Although this technique may seem selfish at first, you must jealously guard your time block. Even if your time management skills are top-notch, keep in mind that the real measure of accomplishment is whether you're moving in a direction that puts you closer to your long-term goals. It's very easy to have a whole lot of motion without any real movement. Or, as Drucker maintains, "It's not enough to do things right. You have to do the right things."

Make A Date With Yourself

The most important appointment on your calendar may be the one you make with yourself. If you find that you consistently put off certain chores, such as filing or catching up on your professional reading, try scheduling a thirty- to sixty-minute "appointment" with yourself. By entering these tasks on your calendar, you may be more likely to tackle them because now they're a priority.

This scheduling technique is particularly helpful if you typically recycle the same "to do" list. Also, making appointments with yourself can be a great stress reliever. Instead of being haunted about the accumulating piles, you have the peace of mind of knowing that you've set aside a specific time to deal with them.

Abandon The "Big Block Belief"

How often, when faced with a big project—say a major speech to write or a lengthy report to read—have you convinced yourself that the only way to start the work is to find a big, disrupted block of time? New research shows that the "big-block belief" may actually make the process more intimidating and prevent you from meeting your deadline.

Robert Boice, a professor of psychology at the State University of New York at Stony Brook, asked ten busy professionals to find a half-hour period each day to work on a major writing project. A second group was allowed to wait to begin the project until they had "enough time" to write. Their progress reports were revealing: Within six months, the professionals instructed to write a half-hour daily were regularly producing nearly four pages a week while the second group on average reported producing less than one-tenth of a page per week.

The secret of the half-hour plunge? Boice concluded it "demystified" the writing process. "We tend to wait for the 'big chunk' of time because we psychologically overvalue writing," he says. "We're convinced it's so difficult that we need forever to do it right."

This principle can be applied to other projects as well. Time management experts have long advocated a theory commonly known as the "Swiss cheese approach." The underlying assumption of this approach is that it's possible to make measurable progress on major projects simply by nibbling away at them. If you've never tried this approach, you may not realize how much you can actually accomplish in a small bite of time. In five minutes, for example, you can organize your steps, possibly identify a shortcut, or select a piece of the project that you can turn over to someone else.

If you're still skeptical, consider these two examples of famous people who knew how to take advantage of spare moments to achieve major goals: Herbert Hoover wrote a book during the time he spent waiting in railroad stations, and Noel Coward wrote his popular song, "I'll See You Again," while caught in a traffic jam.

Monitor Your Meetings

Some managers spend as much as 40 percent of their time attending meetings, according to recent studies. What such surveys rarely reveal—but managers are quick to admit— is that a good many business meetings are unnecessary and unproductive. So why not quit having them? Because meetings are a way of life in many companies and it's not easy to question corporate culture. To cut back on the time you spend in meetings, you can do two things: (1) increase the efficiency of your own meetings and (2) curtail your participation in other people's meetings.

Put Your Own Meetings to the Test

One of the biggest problems with meetings is that people call them out of habit. The next time you're planning a meeting, question its necessity, using this checklist:

✔ *Are the key players available?* It doesn't make sense to call a meeting if all the people responsible for making decisions aren't present. More often than not, this leads to additional meetings.

✔ *Do we have the information necessary for a meaningful discussion?* Lots of meetings turn out to be a waste of time because the participants haven't done their homework. Say, for example, you call a meeting to make a decision about launching a new product, only to discover the cost estimates aren't ready. To prevent a meeting from turning into a reminder session, touch base with participants a day or so in advance to make sure everyone comes prepared.

✔ *Is this meeting an ego trip?* A common complaint of subordinates is that their bosses call meetings just to get strokes. A meeting whose sole purpose is to gather feedback on your ideas and decisions is likely to be deemed a waste of time by participants.

✔ *Could the subject of the meeting be approached in another way?* Many meetings could be replaced by memos. If all you plan to do is impart new information, and not something that needs to be debated, put your ideas on paper.

Participating in Other People's Meetings

Meetings can be frustrating time killers, especially when your attendance is not essential. Chicago business consultant Dina Kerner estimates most managers waste about one-fifth of their time attending meetings where their presence is not really required. "Committee chairmen often invite managers to meetings as a courtesy," says Kerner.

"Sometimes you're included as a precautionary measure to provide information to the group, if the discussion moves in that direction, or because the chairman doesn't want to bother sending out a memo summarizing what happened."

To trim the time you spend in meetings, keep track of all the ones you attend for a month, then decide whether you need to be physically present at future sessions. One way to cut down your attendance is to send an assistant in your place. If you can't avoid a meeting altogether, you may be able to graciously limit your time with these exit techniques advocated by seminar leader Charles Hobbs:

- Ask "Is there any other contribution I can make in this meeting?" If there isn't, most meeting leaders will take the cue and excuse you.
- Simply ask to be excused. If your presence isn't vital, this is a reasonable request that people will honor.
- Arrange to have someone, such as your secretary, interrupt with a reason for you to leave early.

While your ability to contribute to the discussion at hand is a good gauge for determining the need to attend a meeting, consultant Kerner offers this counsel: Don't assume that because you don't speak, your presence at the meeting is unimportant. "Failure to attend a meeting called by the president of the company to set priorities for the firm would be a bad political move," she explains. "He might interpret it as a slight even though you never say anything."

Eliminate Interruptions

The amount of time spent on a project doesn't count—it's the *uninterrupted* time, says time management expert

Bliss. The key is to establish an hour or so of "quiet time" when you refuse to be interrupted, except for emergencies.

But, as we've all experienced, eliminating interruptions is often easier said than done, especially if you're a manager responsible for staff or you operate a business out of your home. Unfortunately, people who are in the habit of popping into your office simply may not realize that they're being disrespectful, cutting into your time, or disturbing your thought process when you're rolling along.

The burden of bringing such intrusions to a halt rests with you. You must establish guidelines to protect your valuable quiet time and communicate those to the people around you. This may sound a bit dictatorial, but in our experience, this is one time management technique that demands a firm hand. Here's how:

First, designate times when you plan to work uninterrupted. Depending on your situation, this could be a set period each day or it may vary according to your projects and deadlines.

The next step is to retrain the people around you. This could be as simple as closing your door to signal that you need some uninterrupted time. If closed doors are discouraged in your work environment, try opening your door partway. This is an effective visitor deterrent that still communicates, "I'm available if needed."

You also can post a sign on your door, such as "available after 10:30." Most people will make an effort not to bother you as long as they know they'll have access to you sometime during the day.

If habitual interrupters still don't get the message, you'll have to be more direct. When someone drops by and asks, "Got a minute?" say politely, "No, not right now. I have something I need to finish." Then graciously offer an alternate time: "How about getting together from 4 to 4:30?" Whatever you say, don't allow yourself to be drawn into a conversation—this will only send a mixed message. You can discourage visitors from settling in for a chat by standing up when they enter your office. Most people recognize this move as a subtle cue that they shouldn't stay long.

If all else fails, simply get away. Move your work to a conference room or library where interrupters can't get at you.

Learn To Say No

Saying no and setting clear priorities are the two most important things top executives do to manage their busy schedules, according to Susan Stautberg and Marcia Worthing, authors of *Balancing Acts* (MasterMedia 1993). "Neither is easy, but both practices are crucial if you are to be an effective manager of time."

Most of us understand the value of setting priorities, but too often we fail to appreciate that our success is determined as much by what we *refuse* to do, as what we choose to do. "If you can learn to combine setting priorities with an increased ability and willingness to say no, you will find that the quality of your work will improve," say Stautberg and Worthing. "You will be working harder on fewer things and concentrating your energies. Your time will be less splintered because you more often will say no to tasks that you don't need to be doing."

Want to increase your ability to say no? Here's what Stautberg and Worthing suggest:

1. Say no immediately, before people can anticipate that you may say yes. Answers such as "I don't know" or "Let me think about it" only get people's hopes up. A delayed no increases the chances of animosity.
2. Realize that you have a right to say no. You don't have to offer a reason every time you turn down someone's request.
3. Offer your refusals politely and pleasantly. There's no need to be defensive—it's your right to say no.
4. Offer a counterproposal if you think it's appropriate and the request is a valid one. "I can't sit in for you at the meeting this afternoon, Joe, but I'll answer your telephone while you are out."

Put An End To Wasted Time

When your lunch date is late, or a meeting doesn't start on time, consider this waiting period a windfall and do something that otherwise would have to wait, suggests Bliss. Always carry a "travel kit" equipped with useful materials such as stationery, stamps, pen, highlighter, pocket recorder, calculator, and your address book. You can also carry along industry reports, magazines, or a book from your reading pile. Being prepared in this way can turn a dreaded delay into an opportunity to get some work done

Says Bliss, "If people keep you waiting, it's your fault, not theirs, if your time is wasted."

PUTTING PAPERWORK
IN PERSPECTIVE

Executives waste an average of four hours a week because they or their assistants can't find things, according to a survey conducted by the San Franciso–based Accountemps, a temporary personnel agency. This adds up to nearly six weeks per year of time wasted in searching for things that are misplaced, misfiled, mislabeled, or just plain gone.

"Today's advanced technologies and services—such as fax machines, electronic mail, overnight delivery, and cellular phones—have increased the pace of business," explains Robert Half, founder of Accountemps. "But they have not resulted in a paperless work environment. Instead, they have increased the volume and flow of information that workers must process."

Paper overload increases the likelihood that important documents will disappear. So when reports, memos, and letters begin to crowd your desk, apply the TRAF system devised by Stephanie Winston, author of *Getting Organized:*

- Trash it;
- Refer or delegate it;
- Act on it; or
- File it.

Using TRAF every time a few papers threaten to grow into an unwieldy stack can save you a lot of frustration and time-consuming searching in the long run.

Master Your Mail

Repeating work you've already done is clearly a waste of time, but that's exactly what many people do when it comes to reading and answering business letters. *Manage Your Time, Manage Your Work, Manage Yourself* authors Merrill E. and Donna N. Douglass advocate an in-today, out-tomorrow approach. Consider your own mail habits. How often do you read a letter, think about how you'd like to answer it, and then set it aside until you have more time to deal with it? The problem with this approach, the Douglasses argue, is that once you go back to the letter, you have to repeat the first two steps all over again.

To prevent mail pile-up, try their in-today, out-tomorrow approach. Handle each letter once: answer it, file it, or discard it. Set aside only those letters that require more information before you can answer them, the Douglasses advise. If you absolutely can't answer a letter after the first reading, at least jot down in the margins any thoughts you have for the response. That way, you won't be starting from square one when you tackle it again later.

Other time-saving mail techniques:
- Eliminate cover letters that don't say anything except "I'm sending you something."
- Keep all letters concise, aiming for a maximum of one paragraph.
- In situations where it's acceptable, don't create a new letter—simply write comments in the margins and return the original to the sender. Joyce regularly uses this method to respond to faxes and other correspondence.

Escape The Reading Trap

If you have a mountain of "must read" materials precariously perched on the corner of your desk and no hope of ever catching up, you're not alone. "We try to read more than is really necessary to stay informed," says Alec Mackenzie, author of *Time for Success: A Goal Getter's Strategy.*

To prevent reading from becoming an overwhelming chore, try "matching the content to your mood," suggests Jacqueline Herrick, a New York financial officer interviewed in the newsletter *Breakthrough Strategies.* Herrick routinely scans headlines in *The Wall Street Journal* and *The New York Times* during her morning train ride because "getting an overview of the news is a good push to get me started."

Herrick saves her heavier reading until after lunch, when she spends about twenty minutes catching up on trade journals, market trends, and other in-depth material. "I find that this reading goes better if I do it midday when my concentration is best, because much of it is complex," she explains. On the commute home, she relaxes with "escapist novels." Sunday nights are saved for books and magazines about finance and management because, Herrick says, after two days of rest, her mind's ready again to tackle something challenging.

If you're facing a backlog of material, here are some techniques to help you clear it out in no time:

Scan the table of contents of day-to-day materials, such as magazines, and read only relevant pages.

Attach a routing slip to publications, placing your name last, and circulate them among your staff, requesting that they note important items and information applicable to your business. By the time the material reaches your desk, you may be able to get most of the information you need simply by reading staff comments.

Preview in-depth material. Say you're trying to tackle a lengthy report. Begin by first flipping through it for ten minutes or so to determine how the material's organized. Are the chapters or sections long, and if so, are they subdivided? Are there lots of diagrams, pictures, and tables? This preview will help you evaluate how much of the material is relevant to you; whether it requires your full concentration, as opposed to a quick skim; and how much time you'll need for the job.

Mark up material that is yours to keep. Underline passages, circle key information, write notes in the margin—anything that will help you find your way through the material and make it useful for future reference. If the material is not yours, photocopy pertinent sections for your own use.

Be a ruthless reader. Skip over material that is repetitious, wordy, or unclear. Even if the topic seems relevant, don't hesitate to bypass a book or article that is so poorly written you find yourself rereading sections in order to grasp the main ideas.

TRIMMING PHONE TIME

The telephone can be an incredible convenience or one of the worst time bandits, depending on how you use it. For instance, making calls to compare prices on a major purchase can save you time and money when you actually go out to shop. On the other hand, feeling compelled to pick up the phone every time it rings can rob you of precious minutes that may be critical in keeping you on schedule.

It's much more efficient to block out a certain time each day to make and receive calls. Let the people you're in contact with regularly know your phone schedule. More importantly, stick to it by letting your answering machine collect messages for any calls you receive outside the phone period you've designated.

As most entrepreneurs who work at home quickly learn, resisting the urge to reach for the phone every few minutes is one of the easiest ways to boost productivity.

Up to one-fourth of the time we spend on the telephone is unproductive, studies show. Yet trimming your telephone time is probably one of the easiest time management techniques to master. Here are some ideas:

To make the most of your time on the phone, outline your conversation before you place a call. Know what you want each call to accomplish, write out the points you want to cover, and decide the amount of time you wish to spend on each. If the other party spends an inordinate amount of time on one point, direct them to the next.

When you place a call and want to get off the phone fast, start by finding out what the other person is doing. For example, asking the person "Did I interrupt you?" might prompt a response such as "No, I was just writing a memo." This clue gives you a convenient but courteous closing. When the objective of the call has been met, say something like, "Okay, I'll let you get back to that memo." Another closing that works well: "Sorry, but I'm going to have to cut this conversation short because I'm expected at a meeting."

When receiving a call, avoid the traditional opening line. Instead of saying "How are you" immediately after greeting a caller, ask "What can I do for you?"

After a caller states their purpose, silently set a time limit for the conversation. Write this on a note you can see as you're talking. If you have difficulty controlling the length of conversations, you may want to monitor yourself using an ordinary kitchen timer.

Avoid being put on hold to wait for someone who's on another line. Instead, request a callback as soon as they finish their first call. If you cannot avoid being put on hold, use the time to do little jobs. For example, open mail, check your schedule, write short notes.

When phoning someone who's long-winded, time your call just before lunch or late in the day. Chances are, they'll be eager to leave. Also, by giving them a reason to keep the conversation short, you avoid any risk of offending talkative acquaintances.

Saving calls for the close of the day is a favorite time-saving technique of Jessica Silberman, a Los Angeles manager interviewed in *Breakthrough Strategies.* Silberman, who receives an average of seventy-five calls every day, has found that postponing her calling hour until 4 P.M. proves productive in more ways than one. "Callers are concise when they receive a call close to 5 P.M.," she explains. "Many early morning callers call back in the afternoon and tell my secretary they don't need to speak to me because they've already taken care of the matter."

Prevent telephone tag by scheduling calls. If you're having trouble connecting with someone, request a specific time to call back. "The very least you should get out of any telephone call is the time the person you are trying to reach will return, or the best time for you to call back," says Nancy Friedman, a St. Louis–based telephone consultant.

If the person you're calling doesn't have a secretary, and you must rely on an answering machine, take the initiative to propose a time for your conversation. For example, say, "I'll call back on Tuesday at 9:45." If a person is interested in your call, they will usually make an effort to be available at that time. Likewise, if you're expecting a return call, leave a message that suggests a time and let the other party know exactly what you want. That way, if you need information that's not readily available, the other party can look it up before returning your call.

Avoid unnecessary call-backs by recapping your conversation. Nothing is more frustrating than hanging up only to realize you need additional information or clarification. That wastes everyone's time. It's a good idea, especially when dealing with hard-to-reach people, to close your conversation by summarizing the content of your call.

Efficiency is integral to good time management. Here are six suggestions designed to turn your telephone into a time-saving tool:

1. Check the location of your phone. Is it within easy reach under normal working conditions? According to some experts, the ideal location is directly on your desk, opposite your writing hand.

2. Develop a system for taking messages. Simple as this sounds, a surprising number of people have to excuse themselves from a conversation to go find a pencil. Whatever system you prefer, whether it's a blackboard, specially designed message tablets, or blank index cards, having your message tools handy will save you a lot of aggravation and create a more positive impression with callers.

3. Post a list of frequently called numbers by the telephone. Better yet, if you have speed dialing, program them into your phone.

4. If you have a business phone that features an automated menu, make sure your greeting gives callers the option of bypassing the complete directory if they simply need to leave a message.

5. Make it a habit to always include your phone number when leaving a message—even if you're calling someone you know has your number. The reason: People whose jobs require them to be out of the office a lot typically call in to check their messages, but may not necessarily have phone numbers handy. Including your number increases your chances of a prompt response.

6. If you rely on voice mail or answering machines to track your calls, make sure your message asks callers to tell you when they need to hear from you. This will help ensure that you return the most urgent calls first.

MINDING YOUR BODY CLOCK

Some of the most productive and creative people in history paid no mind to time in the traditional sense. Pablo Picasso, Thomas Edison, Winston Churchill, and Margaret Mead are among the many geniuses notorious for dozing off at will. While most of us find it difficult to indulge in a midday nap or unusual sleep habits, we do recognize that there are times of the day when we feel most alert and others when our energy lags. Commonly referred to as our "body clock," what we're experiencing are circadian rhythms that control our mental and physical abilities within a 24-hour period. For instance, it's generally true that tasks requiring verbal reasoning and short-term memory are best done in the morning, while most people's long-term memory is sharpest between 6 P.M. and midnight.

Unlike other timepieces, our inner clocks keep an irregular rhythm that may be affected by such forces as sunlight, season, mood, and age. Don't try to resist the calls of your mind and body—they can help you tap your full potential. "You can become more productive by becoming aware of your prime time, the periods of the day when you are physically and mentally at your best," says Dr. Harriet B. Braiker, author of *Type E: The Dilemma of High Achieving Women*. "Some people find early morning best, because they get their energy early in the day. Other people are night hawks, They start out with low energy and concentration, but gradually peak. Others have a burst of energy in the middle of the day and then a slow decline."

You can determine your prime time by taking what Braiker calls a "psychological temperature." Every day for two weeks, take readings at 9 A.M., noon, 3 P.M., 6 P.M., and 9 P.M., by asking yourself these questions:

1. How alert do I feel at this time?
2. How motivated do I feel at this time?
3. How much concentration do I have?
4. How much energy do I have?

Rate your answers on a scale of 1 to 10, with 10 being the highest. After a few days, you should see an energy pattern emerging. The next step is to shift your priorities so you make the best use of your energy peaks and valleys. Here's how:

✔ Schedule your most demanding tasks for those times when you scored high in all four areas— alertness, motivation, concentration, and energy.
✔ Save routine tasks for your low-ebb times.
✔ Look for periods where you can "cheat," by using one factor to overcome a deficit in another. For example, if you typically feel motivated at 3 P.M., but you lose steam physically, try a high-energy task. By focusing on your motivation, you may be able to compensate for a lack of energy.

Become An Early Bird

If you want to feel more in control of your day, try getting up a little earlier. Getting a head start can boost your productivity in several ways:

- Allowing yourself more time to prepare for the day ahead strengthens your confidence.
- An early start helps you avoid the stress and sense of overwork that invariably come from always being late or just barely on time.
- Getting a grip on your schedule—rather than constantly feeling controlled by the day's events—improves your attitude and enables you to cope with challenges in a more positive way.

Tackle The Worst First

For many people, the prospect of an unpleasant task, such as a difficult conversation with a subordinate, has a direct impact on their mood and mind-set. That's why dealing with a disagreeable duty first thing in the day may actually save you time. The reason: With the worst part of your day behind you, your concentration and momentum increase. You also avoid the time-wasting trap of sitting at your desk while you mentally rehearse the upcoming encounter.

TAKING TIME OUT

Sometimes the best way to be productive is to give yourself a break. Ann McGee-Cooper, author of *You Don't Have To*

Go Home From Work Exhausted! observes that "most high energy people typically have hobbies and outside interests that feed new energy and insights into each other." In fact, many of the world's greatest breakthroughs were inspired by hobbies rather than vocations, notes McGee-Cooper: "The Wright brothers ran a bicycle shop but had a passion for flying...Copernicus was an amateur astronomer. Ben Franklin, Thomas Jefferson, and many others made major contributions out of love for their hobbies while making their living in other, more conventional areas."

Many experts advocate the benefits of brief breaks because productivity is not simply a matter of keeping a tight rein on your time. It doesn't hurt to occasionally give yourself permission to get off the treadmill. There are many ways to do this. A hobby is one. A bubble bath is another. So is curling up with a favorite book or taking time out to have a cup of tea while you chat with a friend on the phone for ten minutes. Don't overload your to-do list so that every minute of the day is dedicated to some task. Leaving some unscheduled time gives you breathing room to respond to the unexpected.

As ironic as it may seem, the busier you are, the more you need periodic timeouts. "One of the biggest pitfalls of working long hours is that they can become a way of life," says psychiatrist Dr. Pierre Mornel. "No matter how busy you are, try to maintain a balance. If you have been working extra hard for a while, take a break. Emphasize the personal side by spending more time on recreation. You'll probably find you're not only more productive on the job, but can enjoy your life more."

Control Your Life Through Language

You can gain considerable control over your life simply by the words you choose when responding to daily requests and demands on your time, advise Tony and Robbie Fanning, authors of *Get It All Done and Still Be Human*. For example, saying "There isn't enough time" reinforces an impression that outside influences control your life. A better choice: "That's not how I want to spend my time." Instead of "I'm too busy" say "I don't want to do it." Replace "I don't have time" with "I choose to do other things with my time," and "I can't find the time for it" with "I won't make time."

Subtract Before You Add

Sometimes the hardest person in the world to say no to is yourself. This can create a vicious cycle: Even as you're nagged by a feeling that there's never enough of you to go around, you just can't resist that offer to take on a plum new assignment. If you're one of these people, we suggest you make this simple but effective rule a part of your life: *Subtract before you add.*

In other words, the next time you're tempted to take on a new responsibility, don't say yes until you've considered what you might eliminate from your life to make room for the new activity. This is true, whether you're talking about work or something you want to do just for fun—because either will place demands on your "free" time.

As you take stock, consider all the possibilities. Are there activities you can give up? Deadlines that can be moved? Someone else who can help with the work, thus absorbing some of the pressures? You may be surprised to discover that in many instances, the answer is yes.

Directing your time toward new commitments usually means you have to let go of some old ones. So don't be ashamed to resign from a committee that doesn't really need your input or to remove yourself from a project that is being handled well by others—because the reality is that clogging your schedule with low-priority items does neither you nor your colleagues much good. Practicing the subtraction rule may not make it any easier to say no, but it will, at the very least, help you resist the temptation to automatically say yes.

YOU CAN'T CHANGE THE NUMBER OF HOURS IN THE DAY, but you can do a lot to make the most of the hours you have. Eliminating time wasters can improve the quality of your life, as long as you understand that good time management is not just about working smarter and faster so you can get more done. Sometimes time management means letting go—of beliefs and habits that may be holding you back. Once you decide what's important to you, time management can help you put it all in perspective by increasing your personal productivity, career potential, and peace of mind.

Chapter 12

DO WHAT YOU LOVE:
Are You an Entrepreneur at Heart?

> *Being my own boss is like the plight of
> the caterpillar: When you stay on the
> ground, you see only what's in front of
> you. But if you let yourself grow and
> become a butterfly, you see a world
> of unlimited possibilities.*
> —Janis L. Hahn
> Director, Radiology Relief Inc.

> *If you want to be happy for a year, win
> the lottery. If you want to be happy
> for life, love what you do.*
> —Mary Higgins Clark
> *While My Pretty One Sleeps*

WE COULDN'T END THIS BOOK WITHOUT MAKING A PITCH of our own for the entrepreneurial life. Not only have we personally experienced great satisfaction and success in being business owners, but also, by most accounts, entrepreneurship promises to be one of the more rewarding

271

careers of the nineties. Some business forecasters go so far as to say there's never been a better time to become your own boss.

This much is certain: Between tremendous shifts in our national economy and the reshaping of corporate America, increasing numbers of people are gravitating toward self-employment. Some are making the leap from employee to entrepreneur enthusiastically, others reluctantly; but either way, the reasons they cite are often the same—all things considered, entrepreneurship is the best option open to them.

THE QUIET REVOLUTION

Although government economists have declared the latest U.S. recession over, jobs lost when wave after wave of layoffs and reorganizations swept through the nation's businesses and institutions in the 1980s are not being recreated at the same momentum. By some estimates, we're currently replacing jobs at only about one-quarter of the rate achieved during other post-recession recoveries.

As a result, the ranks of temporary employees and contract workers are growing—not just in the customary trades but in almost all professions. Even within the traditional corporate structure, employment expectations are changing. With so many companies using technology to experiment with new ways of working, such as the "virtual office" and telecommuting, employees are being asked to operate much more independently than in the past.

The bottom line: American workers have started to rethink what it means to make a successful living. For many, especially those whose careers have been sidetracked by downsizing and restructuring, the conventional counsel that "the safest way to make a living is to get a job" no longer rings true.

"People are learning to fend for themselves," observes Edith Weiner, a futurist and author whose books include *Office Biology: Why Tuesday Is The Most Productive Day And Other Relevant Facts For Survival In The Workplace* (MasterMedia, 1993).

"One of the reasons for being employed is to extract long-term promises—for instance, 'You will have a pension here,' 'You will be employed here as long as you produce,' 'Your salary will go up on a regular basis.' But none of those promises are there anymore," Weiner explains. In the face of such upheaval, even people with seemingly secure situations are starting to question their career choices and explore alternatives, which explains in part the growing appeal of self-employment.

The current migration toward entrepreneurialism will continue well into the 21st century, predicts Weiner, who estimates that at least 40 percent of the population will accept responsibility for their own employment. Here's how she traces the evolution of this trend:

"The entrepreneurial mentality was once the exception to the rule in the industrial era—everyone flocked to be employees. In the post-industrial era, our best and brightest were still trained to work for large institutions. In the future, the entrepreneurial mind-set is going to have to be taken up by far larger percentages of the population because the employee entitlement era is gone. It's over, finished."

What we're witnessing is a "quiet revolution," says Barbara Winter in her book *Making a Living Without a Job*. "Business and government leaders used to say, 'What's good for General Motors is good for the country.' But GM is no longer the paragon of American business. And other big businesses have also lost their cachet, as well as the belief that they were the foundation of our society's economic health. Big business is no longer the place where the action is."

Winter, who teaches a seminar on self-employment, maintains that "something is happening in the world of work. People are bravely demanding more. After examining the alternatives, many see that becoming joyfully jobless provides the greatest opportunity for financial, emotional, and even spiritual well-being in their workplace."

Capitalizing On A Hot Career

Regardless of how observers characterize the movement occurring in the workplace, there's no question our views about work and careers are changing in ways that will have a widespread and long-term impact on society and the nation's economy. Even the U.S. Congress has recognized this shift, declaring the 1990s the "Decade of the Entrepreneur." It's no wonder, when study after study confirms that the ranks of the self-employed are multiplying—further evidence that entrepreneurship is increasingly regarded as a hot career:

- More than 20.4 million Americans already operate their own businesses, contributing more than $1 trillion in revenues to our economy and employing nearly 60 percent of American workers.
- Some 39 million Americans do part or all of their work at home—a 56.6 percent increase over the past five years—according to a study by Link Resources, a New York–based research firm.

- Within the next decade, the U.S. Small Business Administration estimates, 60 percent of all families will have some type of home-based business.
- Women are starting new businesses at two to five times the rate of men—by the year 2000, between 40 percent and 50 percent of all businesses will be owned by women.

SETTING NEW STANDARDS FOR SUCCESS

Of the many theories offered for why entrepreneurs have become one of the fastest-growing segments of American workers, one widely accepted explanation is that our priorities have changed. The things we value as a society in the nineties are dramatically different than the desires that drove us at breakneck speed a decade ago. In a *Working Woman* survey of 1,027 adults conducted by the Roper Organization, 53 percent of the men and women polled said their definition of "being successful" had changed in the last five years.

So what do Americans now associate with being successful? At the top of their list: a happy family life or relationship, according to 79 percent of those surveyed. Having enough time for family and friends was second, followed by being in control of their lives. "Asked to choose three out of seven things that would make them feel personally successful, survey respondents ranked the traditional trappings of money, career, and power dead last; 26 percent, 11 percent, and 7 percent, respectively, selected these items," according to *Working Woman*.

Ironically, our notion of success seems to have broadened because our career options—in the classic sense of constantly moving up and earning more—have narrowed. The survey findings "show that the go-go era of the eighties is dead," concludes Nicholas Tortorello, senior vice president at Roper. "When everything unraveled, people changed their definitions of success from having money to being liked by other people to having a role in the community. We're a nation that likes to be optimistic, and the definition we've changed to is more attainable and reasonable."

Likewise, the sacrifices many of us once made routinely, almost unthinkingly, are no longer considered part of the bargain. Instead, people are happily forfeiting the prestige of a corporate office and relinquishing the promise of a regular paycheck in favor of having more say in determining the direction of their lives. "Success, for me, is having the freedom to decide what success is," Barbara Alpert, a New Yorker who owns a television production company with her husband, told *Working Woman*. "It's about doing what I want to do. It's not about meeting other people's expectations."

Similar sentiments were echoed in a survey by *Home Office Computing*. The magazine's readers cited a number of advantages in abandoning the nine-to-five world. Among the more telling: 98 percent said they were happier in general; 96 percent would recommend working from home; and 88 percent said they would never return to the corporate world. Other noteworthy responses:

- 85 percent felt more relaxed working at home;
- 40 percent enjoyed a healthier diet;
- 39 percent took more time off; and
- 38 percent exercised more often.

A Different Breed

Entrepreneurs are clearly a breed apart—they're the "new aristocracy," says Hugh Roome, publisher of *Home Office Computing.* "The small- or home-office entrepreneur possesses a level of freedom of action that was, until recently, the exclusive preserve of the very wealthy."

Writing in his monthly letter to the magazine's readers, Roome observes, "Interestingly, it was once thought that lawyers, doctors, bankers, and corporate chieftains would comprise the aristocracy of the late 20th century, as they had done in the generation before. But the pace of life today for these men and women just doesn't afford them the time to think and choose. They are imprisoned by the fast track...as an entrepreneur, you are in the distinguished position of having ready access to distinct freedoms while the vast majority are trapped in traditional work and home patterns. Yours is a lifestyle unique to your generation."

Here's how Roome portrays the particular freedoms that entrepreneurs enjoy:

Time. Entrepreneurs, unlike their corporate counterparts, can determine how they will spend their time. As independent business owners, they can manage their own destiny and balance the trade-offs among family, work, entertainment, and community responsibilities.

Geographic freedom. Small- and home-offices, because they can be electronically linked to customers and the world at large, have the freedom to be located wherever you choose to place them.

Financial freedom. Although you may feel that you're more focused on money to provide for your basic needs than you were while working in a corporate environment, the fact is that, as an entrepreneur, you have the ability to determine your own fate in this regard.

Communications freedom. Like the aristocracy of the old, the small- and home-office elite have distinct communications mechanisms that are not available to most of society—online access, for instance, is a vital aspect of the information elite.

EXPLORING ENTREPRENEURIAL OPPORTUNITIES

As appealing as the entrepreneurial life may sound, the truth is, starting your own business is one of the riskier career moves you can make. But if you have a hankering to be your own boss, now's the time to do it, most experts advise. "The demand for things that small businesses are best at providing—such as paying attention to customers' individual needs, the flexibility to respond quickly to changes, and efficient service—has never been higher," says Geoffrey Kessler, of the Kessler Exchange, a California-based small-business research firm.

Many entrepreneurs get their start because in a flash of inspiration—which they often equate with a light bulb going on—they suddenly see a way to turn everyday experience into a fresh opportunity. In today's fast-paced world, new businesses are being born every day by would-be entrepreneurs who've dreamed up yet another product or service to meet society's ever-changing needs.

Some promising markets for new entrepreneurs:
- entertainment
- education and training
- environmental products and services
- health care (mental, physical, cosmetic)
- products and services for children or seniors (because baby boomers are now taking care of both)
- spiritual enhancement
- ethnic-related concepts
- security services (financial and personal safety)

Making The Leap

If you've ever wished you could fuse your personal and professional interests into a career, or you daydream of being your own boss, or you long to bound out of bed in the morning, knowing your day will be spent doing work you love, you obviously have entrepreneurial leanings. But that doesn't necessarily mean you have the makings of a business owner.

While we would be the first to encourage you to explore your entrepreneurial inclinations, we can't overemphasize the need to carefully evaluate all your career options before making the leap to self-employment—because as exhilarating as business ownership can be, there are certainly easier ways to make a living. Even the most successful entrepreneurs caution that running your own business, however large or small, is an all-consuming career that touches on every aspect of your life. As Winter so aptly sums it up: "Being your own boss is both heady and humbling, but it's seldom boring."

Finding The Right Fit

Finding meaningful work, a career that "fits," happens naturally for some people. At an early age, they're struck with a vision of what they want to be when they grow up and that becomes their guiding passion. But for most of us, the process is more like a journey in which we sample several jobs, and maybe even explore different career paths and professions, before we reach our destination and can honestly say we've found the work we were meant to do in life. While the journey can be discouraging, anyone who's found their fit—a career where professional and personal passions merge—will tell you it's the only way to achieve long-term fulfillment.

"When you are doing work you love, all else in life seems to fall into place," says Nancy Anderson, a career consultant and author of *Work with Passion.* "It is through the dignity of the work we do that we achieve self-esteem in life."

Career studies show that the two most important factors in finding your fit are:

1. Doing something that makes you feel good about yourself; and
2. Doing something that enables you to contribute or make a positive difference.

Entrepreneurs, as we've said, are a special breed. Unlike people who work because they need to earn a paycheck, entrepreneurs are driven by a personal vision. When they talk about their life's work, they typically describe it in reverent, almost spiritual, terms. "Being in business is not about making money," says Paul Hawken, author of *Growing A Business.* "It is a way to become who you are." Similarly, Harvey Mackay, a successful entrepreneur who rose to best-sellerdom with business books such as *Swim with the Sharks Without Being Eaten Alive,* puts it this way: "If you find something you love to do, you'll never have to work again for the rest of your life."

Are You Cut Out To Be Your Own Boss?

Though many people are initially drawn to the entrepreneurial life because of the independence and freedom it offers, not everyone is cut out to be their own boss. Entrepreneurs must master a range of skills that is at times overwhelming, not to mention the responsibility they shoulder on a day-to-day basis.

So how do you know if you have what it takes to run your own business? Successful self-bossers are typically high-spirited, strong-minded individuals who, specific professional skills aside, share some common traits. Entrepreneurs
* possess the ability to see value where others do not;
* have the courage to be different;
* are not intimidated by difficult, unknown situations;
* adapt to change and capitalize on it;
* learn how to deal with failure as a way of learning;
* are calculating risk-takers—they're not afraid to take a chance, but they typically work like demons to get the odds on their side;

- have a passionate desire to grow;
- are oriented toward opportunities and goals—
  they believe it's better to have a great idea and
  no money, than millions and no idea;
- have a fierce determination to succeed; and
- appreciate the importance of sales and believe in
  promoting their ideas.

Marrying Passion With Profit

If you've found your passion and feel you having the makings of an entrepreneur, it's time to get down to business. While your first impulse may be to set up shop, you're better off investing your energy in research to ensure that your passion has potential as a profit-making venture.

"Try to get your hands on people who have done exactly what you want to do," advises Mackay. "Ask them what they would do differently if they had to start over again. Listen, take copious notes, and thank them with a beautiful follow-up note. Get a mentor if you can. Read everything there is to read. If you get only one good idea from every book or article, it's time well spent."

Mackay also advocates seeking a second opinion from an industrial psychologist before you set up shop. "You go and take four hours of tests and find out your strengths, weaknesses, what you are truly interested in. It's not cheap, but it can steer you away from a bad decision toward a better one."

There's no limit to the expert counsel that's available, if you're willing to do a little legwork to track down the resources in your area. Many colleges now offer specialized courses and even degree programs for entrepreneurs. On a smaller scale, there are any number of workshops and seminars designed to help you explore various aspects of entrepreneurship. "Making a Living Without a Job," by Barbara Winter, who we've quoted frequently, is one such seminar.

Another source is Avon Products, the international cosmetics company that has been fostering entrepreneurship among women since 1886, when it recruited its first sales representative. Wanting to share more than a century of expertise and insight, the company developed a workshop for women called "Take Control of Your Life: Start Your Own Business."

Among the advice offered at the workshop, participants receive a booklet titled *Ten Practical Steps To Get You Started,* which, in our view, is one of the most succinct yet insightful overviews available on the subject of becoming an entrepreneur. We've excerpted portions of the booklet here, courtesy of Avon.

Starting a business doesn't happen overnight. It requires careful planning and well-thought-out strategies. We've put together ten steps to help you get started. Think of each step as a stage in your development as an entrepreneur, stages every successful business owner has gone through to make their dream a reality.

STEP #1
Develop Your Confidence

Self-confidence is at the heart of your ability to turn your dream of self-employment into a viable business. It fuels the drive, determination, and dedication demanded of an entrepreneur to overcome the personal and financial challenges faced when getting started.

Develop confidence from within: Believe in yourself and your ability to succeed. You must be your No. 1 fan, cheering yourself to the finish line.

Have a positive attitude: If you think positively, you'll act positively—doing what it takes to get your business off the ground. Each new accomplishment will add to your confidence and enhance your positive approach.

Nurture your self-confidence: Build an external support network. Recognize that every so often you'll need a booster shot of confidence to keep your spirits up and rekindle your enthusiasm.

STEP #2
Define Your Goals

Before you can begin to fill in the details of setting up shop, draw the outline of your new life as a business owner by defining your long-term and short-term goals.

Starting your own business involves more than providing a service or product for money; it's about the way you want to live your life. Defining your personal goals helps you build a business to fit into your life and enable you to meet these goals. As you reach each goal, replace it with a new one. This is the mark of a true entrepreneur.

To focus your ideas, answer these questions:
• Where am I now and what do I want
  from my life?
• What kind of lifestyle do I want to lead?

- How much money do I need to earn to achieve this lifestyle?
- What kind of person do I want to be?
- How do I want the people in my life to think of me?

STEP #3
Assess Yourself as an Entrepreneur

The first question that comes to anyone's mind when considering business ownership is: Do I have what it takes to become a successful entrepreneur? Running a business requires certain skills and characteristics you already have or will develop.

When you evaluate yourself, be honest. Much of your success will depend on how well you know your limitations and strengths. Generally, you'll need to rely on these personality traits common to successful entrepreneurs:

Independence. You have only yourself to depend on to take care of projects, resolve problems, and accept responsibility for your actions.

Self-discipline. You're your own boss, so it'll be up to you to stay on top of your workload and get things done.

Creativity. You'll be handling responsibilities new to you, so you'll need to learn how to think on your feet and come up with ways to deal decisively with various situations.

Drive and determination. Starting a business takes a lot of hard work, initiative, and commitment of time beyond the conventional forty-hour work week.

Tolerance for risk. There is no guaranteed paycheck or company benefits to fall back on. You'll always have to live with some degree of financial insecurity.

Confidence. You'll have to make you own decisions and be assured enough not to second-guess yourself. At the same time, you'll need to bounce back when you've make mistakes.

STEP #4
Find the Right Business

What businesses are people starting? Every kind imaginable—from manufacturing to service, from franchising to direct selling. The challenge is to discover which one is best for you.

Start by analyzing your background to determine your skills, interests, and experiences. You'll increase your chances for success if you choose a business that builds on your strengths.

Once you have an idea about what business you'd like to establish, do market research. The more thorough your up-front research, the better prepared you'll be to ask the right questions and make the right decisions.

Keep it simple. In the business world, you have to walk before you can run, so

- start small, to cut down on risks and start-up costs.

- learn as you go without a big investment up front.
- rule out business ideas that need expensive equipment or machinery, high-priced office space, or a large staff to get under way.
- grow your business sensibly, based on profit growth, market demand, and the amount of time and energy you can invest.

STEP #5
Choose the Best Approach

Your choice of business will depend in large part on your personal goals, your resources, and the money you need to earn. Here are some options:
- Set up a home-based business.
- Buy an existing business.
- Be an independent contractor.
- Open a franchise.

STEP #6
Develop a Business Plan

A carefully constructed, comprehensive business plan serves as the blueprint for your business. It forces you to focus on each aspect of setting up and running your business, it is your plan of action, and it serves as the basis for a presentation or proposal you might need to obtain outside financing. Overall, a business plan helps you
- define your business, customers, and competition;
- set long- and short-term goals;
- determine exactly what information you'll need to start your business;

- discover any changes to be made before you expand your business; and
- understand what it will take to begin your business before you invest more time and money.

STEP #7
Get Help From Experts

Even the smallest and newest business enterprises need help from specialists for start-up and growth. There are experts available to assist you with each aspect of your business, from financial advisors to public relations consultants.

Do your homework before setting up meetings and incurring costs. Don't go for help until you understand the general issues and professional terminology that will form the basis of your discussion. Be informed when you seek help so you can ask the right questions and evaluate the soundness of the advice given.

Once you've selected advisors, make sure you establish an ongoing working relationship with them. Be honest and open. Remember, they're on your side—it is in their best interests to see you succeed.

STEP #8
Line Up Financing

How much money you'll need for start-up will depend on the equipment, supplies, and space requirements for your business. Have a cash reserve to cover your operating expenses for at least one year. Insufficient start-up funds and working capital are a principal cause of business failure, so it's imperative to sit down with an accountant or consultant to determine your needs.

Don't be intimidated by financial jargon. Acquire the habit of reading business newspapers and publications and purchase a dictionary of business terms to learn the language. Once you've established your business, you'll need to keep on top of general business trends.

Sources of financing generally available to start up a business include:
- prospective owner, family, and friends;
- banks;
- commercial finance companies;
- venture capital funds;
- state and federal funding programs; and
- local development companies.

STEP #9
Get Organized

In addition to your business, other aspects of your life will make demands on your time and energy. You'll have to work hard at organizing your business life and your personal life to achieve a healthy balance. Once you take control of your life, it becomes much easier to juggle responsibilities as a business owner, parent, spouse, and friend.

Organize your work space. Don't confuse being organized with merely being neat. Being organized means having a system for arranging files, materials, supplies, and everything else you'll need.

Manage your time. Plan your day's activities carefully, taking into consideration your personal, business, and family needs. While being your own boss gives you flexibility in planning to meet these needs, you must be conducting business when the rest of the business world, including your customers and suppliers, is at work.

STEP #10
Take a Deep Breath and Go For It!

Starting a business takes considerable energy, time, and resources, but with prudent planning and a confident attitude, you can join the millions of people who have become successful business owners.

Use your resources. In planning your business, start out with the attitude that for every problem you encounter, you can find the information you need to solve it. Some of your best sources include the public library, organizations, trade associations, government resources, and community colleges.

Conquer cold feet. As you face the prospect of self-employment, no doubt some feelings of insecurity are growing inside you. Be encouraged by the fact that an overwhelming majority of entrepreneurs believe that the rewards of business ownership far outweigh the risks and challenges.

Keep well. Above all, take good care of yourself. You will be the most important commodity in your business. Remember, because you represent your business, the way you look makes a difference. If you feel good about yourself, the people you meet will feel the same. Do the things you need to do to enhance your well-being—physically, intellectually, and spiritually. You'll find these investments will pay off in the way you approach your business and take control of your life.

LIFE'S TOO SHORT NOT TO DO WHAT YOU LOVE

If you know in your heart and mind that what you really want to be is an entrepreneur, don't let anyone or anything discourage you from pursuing your dreams. While it's important to exercise caution when making such a major change in your life's direction, be aware that if you wait for the perfect moment, you'll probably never make the leap to self-employment. Accept the fact that whenever you do, you'll have to confront naysayers and meet challenges such as a tenuous economy. Bottom line, there's never a bad time to start your own business—as long as you have a good idea and sound research to back it up.

"Sometimes the worst of times are the best of times," observes Mackay. Why? "In tough times, a lot of your competition has already given up, leaving you the opportunity."

His advice to would-be entrepreneurs: "If you have gathered the information you need and you know your business idea has potential, but you still haven't decided whether to take the leap, you should know one thing—I have never, and let me emphasize never, met anyone who has gone out on his own, who has taken a crack at it, even if he failed, who has been sorry he did it."

We couldn't agree more.

IT'S SO EASY TO GET CAUGHT UP IN THE DAILY GRIND that too few of us stop to really consider whether we like what we do and why it gives us satisfaction. From time to time, we all need to step back and reassess our lives. If you can't honestly say that you love what you do, if you're only going through the motions, we'd like to suggest that some serious soul-searching and healthy personal upheaval are in order.

And, if you have an urge to completely reinvent yourself, but haven't yet summoned up the courage to take the first step, remember, risk-takers invariably reap the biggest rewards. That's what "selling yourself" is all about—getting out there and going after what you want with all the passion and poise you possess. We did it, and so can you!

About the Authors

As a young girl, Kathy Thebo was so painfully shy that she once opted to take a "D" grade—and ruin her "A" average—rather than deliver an oral report. In fact, the very thought of addressing her classmates provoked an almost physical paralysis.

Today, Thebo is a top sales representative for Avon Products, Inc. Polished and articulate, she enjoys financial and social success that have made her a role model among her peers. Often in demand as a keynote speaker, Thebo engages audiences with her enthusiasm and inspires them with the story of her metamorphosis. She's appeared on national TV and been featured in major magazines. Thebo lives in Peoria, Arizona, with her four children.

Joyce Newman's career has been dedicated to helping professionals improve their communications and presentation skills. A coach to celebrities and CEOs alike, Newman employs a caring approach that focuses on accentuating the positive qualities in clients who seek her expert counsel when preparing for public appearances ranging from business meetings to book tours to television talk shows.

A talented speaker herself, Newman frequently addresses industry and association conferences on such topics as "Power Speaking" and "Managing the Media."

Widely recognized as an authority on communications, Newman maintains an international clientele that includes such companies as Amdahl Corporation, the Bear Stearns Companies, BBDO Worldwide, Booz•Allen Hamilton Inc., Bristol-Myers Squibb International, Canadian Imperial Bank of Commerce, MCI Telecommunications Corporation, Simon & Schuster, and Time-Warner Inc., as well as many celebrity spokespeople, such as Chris Evert, Mickey Mantle, Randy Travis, Scott Hamilton, and Emerson Fittipaldi.

Newman has authored or been featured in numerous articles related to her expertise. Married, with a daughter, she lives in New York City.

DIANA LYNN IS AN AWARD-WINNING JOURNALIST AND BUSINESS communicator with more than a decade of editorial and management experience in newspapers, corporate communications, and publishing. Now an entrepreneur, she heads her own New York City–based electronic publishing and communications consulting firm. This is her third book.

Additional copies of *Selling Yourself* may be ordered by sending a check for $12.95 (please add $2 postage and handling for the first copy, $1 for each additional copy) to

MasterMedia Limited
17 East 89th Street
New York, NY 10128
(800) 334-8232, (212) 260-5600
Fax (212) 546-7638

The authors are available for workshops, seminars, and speeches. Please contact MasterMedia's Speakers' Bureau for availability and fee arrangements. Call Tony Colao at (800) 453- 2887 or fax (908) 359-1647.

OTHER MASTERMEDIA BOOKS

At bookstores, or call (800) 334-8232 to place a credit card order.

BALANCING ACTS! Juggling Love, Work, Family, and Recreation, by Susan Stautberg and Marcia Worthing, provides strategies to achieve a balanced life by reordering priorities and setting realistic goals. ($12.95 paper)

BEATING THE AGE GAME: Redefining Retirement, by Jack and Phoebe Ballard, debunks the myth that retirement means sitting out the rest of the game. The years between 55 and 80 can be your best, say the authors, who provide ample examples of people successfully using retirement to reinvent their lives. ($12.95 paper)

THE BIG APPLE BUSINESS AND PLEASURE GUIDE: 501 Ways To Work Smarter, Play Harder, and Live Better in New York City, by Muriel Siebert and Susan Kleinman, offers visitors and New Yorkers alike advice on how to do business in the city and enjoy its attractions. ($9.95 paper)

BOUNCING BACK: How to Turn Business Crises into Success, by Harvey Reese. Based on interviews with entrepreneurs, Reese has discovered a formula for success that is a must read. ($18.95 cloth)

CARVING WOOD AND STONE, by Arnold Prince, is an illustrated step-by-step handbook demonstrating all you need to hone your wood and carving skills. ($15.95 paper)

THE COLLEGE COOKBOOK II, For Students by Students, by Nancy Levicki, is a handy volume of recipes culled from college students across the country. (11.95 paper)

THE CONFIDENCE FACTOR: How Self-Esteem Can Change Your Life, by Dr. Judith Briles, is based on a nationwide survey of 6000 men and women. Briles explores why women often feel a lack of self-confidence and have a poor opinion of themselves. She offers step-by-step advice on becoming the person you want to be. ($12.95 paper, $18.95 cloth)

CUPID, COUPLES & CONTRACTS: A Guide to Living Together, Prenuptial Agreements, and Divorce, by Lester Wallman, with Sharon McDonnell, is an insightful, consumer-oriented handbook that provides a comprehensive overview of family law, including prenuptial agreements, alimony, and fathers' rights. ($12.95 paper)

THE DOLLARS AND SENSE OF DIVORCE: The Financial Guide for Women, by Dr. Judith Briles, is the first book to combine the legal hurdles by planning finances before, during, and after divorce. ($10.95 paper)

FINANCIAL SAVVY FOR WOMEN: A Money Book for Women of All Ages, by Dr. Judith Briles, divides a woman's monetary lifespan into six phases, discusses specific issues to be addressed at each stage, and demonstrates how to create a sound money plan. ($15.00 paper)

FLIGHT PLAN FOR LIVING: The Art of Self-Encouragement, by Patrick O'Dooley, is a guide organized like a pilot's checklist, to ensure you'll be flying "clear on top" throughout your life. ($17.95 cloth)

HERITAGE, The Making of the American Family, by Robert Pamplin Jr., Gary Eisler, Jeff Sengstack, and John Domini, mixes history and philosophy in a biographical saga of the Pamplins' phenomemal ascent to wealth and the creation of one of the largest private fortunes in the U.S. ($24.95 cloth)

HOT HEALTH-CARE CAREERS, by Margaret McNally and Phyllis Schneider, offers readers what they need to know about training for and getting jobs in a rewarding field where professionals are always in demand. ($10.95 paper)

HOW NOT TO GET FIRED: Ten Steps to Becoming an Indispensable Employee, by Carole Hyatt, shows readers how to take a fresh look at their career paths, adapt to the current marketplace by using old skills in new ways, and discover options they didn't know they had. ($12.95 paper)

HOW TO GET WHAT YOU WANT FROM ALMOST ANYBODY, by T. Scott Gross, shows how to get great service, negotiate better prices, and always get what you pay for. ($9.95 paper)

KIDS WHO MAKE A DIFFERENCE, by Joyce Roché and Marie Rodriguez, is an inspiring document of how today's toughest challenges are being met by teenagers and kids, whose courage and creativity enables them to find practical solutions! ($8.95 paper, with photos)

LEADING YOUR POSITIVELY OUTRAGEOUS SERVICE TEAM, by T. Scott Gross, forgoes theory in favor of a hands-on approach, Gross providing a step-by-step formula for developing self-managing service teams that put the customer first. ($12.95 paper)

LIFE'S THIRD ACT: Taking Control of Your Mature Years, by Patricia Burnham, Ph.D., is a perceptive handbook for everyone who recognizes that planning is the key to enjoying your mature years. ($18.95 cloth)

LISTEN TO WIN: A Guide to Effective Listening, by Curt Bechler and Richard Weaver, Ph.D.s, is a powerful, people-oriented book that will help you learn to live with others, connect with them, get the best from them, and empower them. ($18.95 cloth)

THE LIVING HEART BRAND NAME SHOPPER'S GUIDE, (3d edition) by Michael DeBakey, M.D., Antonio Gotto, Jr., M.D., Lynne Scott, M.A., R.D./L.D., and John Foreyt, Ph.D., lists brand name products low in fat, saturated fatty acids, and cholesterol ($14.95 paper)

THE LIVING HEART GUIDE TO EATING OUT, by Michael E. DeBakey, Antonio M. Gotto, Jr., and Lynne W. Scott, is an essential handbook for people who want to maintain a health-conscious diet when dining in all types of restaurants. ($9.95 paper)

MAKING YOUR DREAMS COME TRUE: A Plan For Easily Discovering and Achieving the Life You Want, by Marcia Wieder, introduces an easy, unique, and practical technique for defining, pursuing, and realizing your career and life interests. Filled with stories of real people and helpful exercises, plus a personal workbook. ($9.95 paper)

MANAGING YOUR CHILD'S DIABETES, by Robert Wood Johnson IV, Sale Johnson, Casey Johnson, and Susan Kleinman, brings help to families trying to understand diabetes and control its effects. Also available in Spanish. ($12.95 paper)

MANAGING YOUR PSORIASIS, by Nicholas J. Lowe, M.D., is an innovative manual that couples scientific research and encouraging support, with an emphasis on how patients can take charge of their health. ($10.95 paper, $17.95 cloth)

MANN FOR ALL SEASONS: Wit and Wisdom from The Washington Post's *Judy Mann,* shows the columnist at her best as she writes about women, families, and the impact and politics of the women's revolution. ($9.95 paper, $19.95 cloth)

MIND YOUR OWN BUSINESS: And Keep it in the Family, by Marcy Syms, CEO of Syms Corp, is an effective guide for any organization facing the toughest step in managing a family business—making the transition to the new generation. ($12.95 paper, $18.95 cloth)

OFFICE BIOLOGY: Why Tuesday Is the Most Productive Day and Other Relevant Facts for Survival in the Workplace, by Edith Weiner and Arnold Brown, teaches how in the '90s and beyond we will be expected to work smarter, take better control of our health, adapt to advancing technology, and improve our lives in ways that are not too costly or resource-intensive. ($12.95 paper, $21.95 cloth)

ON TARGET: Enhance Your Life and Advance Your Career, by Jeri Sedlar and Rick Miners, is a neatly woven tapestry of insights on career and life issues gathered from audiences across the country. This feedback has been crystallized into a highly readable guide for exploring who you are and how to go about getting what you want. ($11.95 paper)

PAIN RELIEF: How to Say No to Acute, Chronic, and Cancer Pain! by Dr. Jane Cowles, offers a step-by-step plan for assessing pain and communicating it to your doctor, and explains the importance of having a pain plan before undergoing any medical or surgical treatment; includes "The Pain Patient's Bill of Rights," and a reusable pain assessment chart. ($14.95 paper, $22.95 cloth)

POSITIVELY OUTRAGEOUS SERVICE: New and Easy Ways To Win Customers for Life, by T. Scott Gross, identifies what '90s consumers really want and how business can develop effective marketing strategies to answer those needs. ($14.95 paper)

POSITIVELY OUTRAGEOUS SERVICE AND SHOWMANSHIP, by T. Scott Gross, reveals the secrets of adding personality to any product or service and offers a wealth of nontraditional marketing techniques employed by top showpeople, from car dealers to restaurateurs, amusement park operators to evangelists. ($12.95 paper)

THE PREGNANCY AND MOTHERHOOD DIARY: Planning the First Year of Your Second Career, by Susan Stautberg, is the only undated appointment diary that shows how to manage pregnancy and career. *Revised and updated.* ($12.95 spiralbound)

REAL BEAUTY...REAL WOMEN: A Handbook for Making the Best of Your Own Good Looks, by Kathleen Walas, international beauty and fashion director of Avon Products Inc., offers expert advice on beauty and fashion for women of all ages and ethnic backgrounds. ($19.50 paper)

ROSEY GRIER'S ALL-AMERICAN HEROES: Multicultural Success Stories, by Roosevelt "Rosey" Grier, is a candid collection of profiles of prominent African Americans, Latins, Asians, and Native

Americans who revealed how they achieved public acclaim and personal success. ($9.95 paper, with photos)

SHOCKWAVES: The Global Impact of Sexual Harassment, by Susan L. Webb, examines the problem of sexual harassment today in every kind of workplace around the world. Practical and well-researched, this manual provides the most recent information available, including legal changes in progress. ($11.95 paper, $19.95 cloth)

SOMEONE ELSE'S SON, by Alan Winter, explores the parent-child bond in a contemporary novel of lost identities, family secrets, and relationships gone awry. Eighteen years after bringing their first son home from the hospital, Trish and Brad Hunter discover they are not his biological parents. ($18.95 cloth)

STEP FORWARD: Sexual Harassment in the Workplace, by Susan L. Webb, presents the facts for dealing with sexual harassment on the job. ($9.95 paper)

THE STEPPARENT CHALLENGE: A Primer For Making It Work, by Stephen Williams, Ph.D., offers insight into the many aspects of step relationships—from financial issues to lifestyle changes to differences in race or religion that affect the whole family. ($13.95 paper)

STRAIGHT TALK ON WOMEN'S HEALTH: How to Get the Health Care You Deserve, by Janice Teal, Ph.D., and Phyllis Schneider, is destined to become a health-care "bible." Devoid of confusing medical jargon, it offers a wealth of resources, including contact lists of healthlines and women's medical centers. ($14.95 paper)

TEAMBUILT: Making Teamwork Work, by Mark Sanborn, teaches businesses how to increase productivity, without increasing resources or expenses, by building teamwork among employees. ($12.95 paper, $19.95 cloth)

A TEEN'S GUIDE TO BUSINESS: The Secrets to a Successful Enterprise, by Linda Menzies, Oren Jenkins, and Rick Fisher, provides solid information about starting your own business or working for one. ($7.95 paper)

WHAT KIDS LIKE TO DO, by Edward Stautberg, Gail Wubbenhorst, Atiya Easterling, and Phyllis Schneider, is a handy guide for parents, grandparents, and baby sitters. Written by kids for kids, this is an easy-to-read, generously illustrated primer for teaching families how to make every day more fun. ($7.95 paper)

WHEN THE WRONG THING IS RIGHT: How to Overcome Conventional Wisdom, Popular Opinion, and All the Lies Your Parents Told You, by Sylvia Bigelsen, Ed.S., and Virginia McCullough, addresses issues such as marriage, relationships, parents and siblings, divorce, sex, money, and careers and encourages readers to break free from the pressures of common wisdom and to trust their own choices.($9.95 paper)

A WOMAN'S PLACE IS EVERYWHERE: Inspirational Profiles of Female Leaders Who Are Expanding the Roles of American Women, by Lindsey Johnson and Jackie Joyner-Kersee, profiles thirty women whose personal and professional achievements are helping to shape and expand our ideas of what's possible for humankind. ($9.95 paper)

YOUR VISION: All About Modern Eye Care, by Warren D. Cross Jr., M.D., and Lawrence Lynn, Ph.D., reveals astounding research discoveries in an entertaining and informative handbook written with the patient in mind. ($13.95 paper, $19.95 cloth)